Jesus, King of Strangers

Jesus, King of Strangers

What the Bible *Really* Says about Immigration

Mark W. Hamilton

WILLIAM B. EERDMANS PUBLISHING COMPANY

GRAND RAPIDS, MICHIGAN

Wm. B. Eerdmans Publishing Co.
4035 Park East Court SE, Grand Rapids, Michigan 49546
www.eerdmans.com

25 24 23 22 21 20 19   1 2 3 4 5 6 7

ISBN 978-0-8028-7662-1

Library of Congress Cataloging-in-Publication Data

A catalog record for this book is available from the Library of Congress.

Contents

malibu
labor
exchange
↓
vcc charity

the exodus — journey
of a migrant

Foreword by Shaun Casey   vii

Preface   xi

1. The Reality of Migration   1

2. The Bible and the Migrant   14

3. Migration as Experience and Literary Theme   30

4. Exodus and Exile   46

5. Exodus, Exile, and Human Nature   63

6. The Law of the Stranger   81

7. The Voice of Prophecy   98

8. Israel as Migrant and Host of Migrants   112

CONTENTS

9. New Testament Transformations   124

10. A Conclusion for Now   141

   Notes   147
   Bibliography   159
   Index   167

Foreword

I T IS A RARE THING when a biblical scholar, at the top of his or her scholarly game, writes a book that compellingly addresses a contemporary political and moral issue as contentious as the current debate in the United States over immigration and refugees. Rarer still is the book that supplants all previous scholarly attempts to cover the same terrain. And rarest of all is a book that displays elegant prose and a strong, clear, and accessible argument comprehensible beyond a small circle of scholars such that a radical book for a wider public emerges. Mark Hamilton's work, *Jesus, King of Strangers*, is one of those once-in-a-generation books that manages to do all these things.

Why should you read this book? Given the fact that certain tribes of American Christianity seem hell-bent on despising, and not loving, their neighbors, at least the ones not born here, all Christians need to take up the argument of this book. To put it bluntly, the way in which American Christians sort the new global reality of hundreds of millions of people on the move may decide the fate many such people face today. People of the Book matter in this controversy. If we Christians turn our backs, America turns its back. If we embrace the migrant and the refugee, the rest of the nation may do likewise. So why not invest a modest amount of time reading a guide to what the Hebrew Bible actually claims about how such people on the move are to be treated?

Scholars, teachers, students, clergy—even presidents—would learn more than a little from *Jesus, King of Strangers*, to say nothing of the sycophantic Christian court prophets who speak smooth and reassuring words of neglect to the current occupant of the White House. As the author argues, many, perhaps most Americans who turn to the Hebrew Bible for some sort of normative guidance have not grasped the full import of that text for the contemporary discussion.

But a much a larger audience should wrestle with the powerful conclusions Mark Hamilton draws. And that audience would be all of us who live in America, be they citizens, resident aliens, visitors, guests, religious, nonreligious, young, old, or undocumented. That is because we all have a stake in how our country sorts the questions around migration and refugee resettlement. The very substance of our democracy is at stake in the face of unprecedented numbers of people on the move around our planet. Will Americans turn their backs to those in need or will we, in league with the rest of the world, do our part to respond in love and help to the most vulnerable around the planet who are fleeing violence, famine, and oppression?

The true power of this book unfolds in a cumulative fashion. Hamilton guides us through the pervasive and central accounts of human movement in the pages of the Bible. People have been traveling across the world throughout human history and they continue today in record numbers. The centrality of human movement in Scripture seems to have eluded our understanding as we current readers of the Bible seem to be blind to this fact. The biblical accounts are not neutral! Hamilton deftly shows us throughout the various literary forms and historical periods woven into the Bible that a compelling set of conclusions emerges. If we accept these accounts as authoritative, our blindness, or worse yet, our repudiation of the truths presented cannot be excused.

The fate of the millions of humans who are currently displaced around the planet is one of the most compelling moral questions of our day. Facing the irony of a country, now populated by descendants of those who came here from other countries, some by choice, others by compulsion, turning its back on the contemporary waves of migrants and refugees is indeed a bitter prospect. We in America are at a moral inflection point, to use contemporary jargon. Will we welcome these people in peril, or will we ignore their pleas for help, shelter, and food in order to maintain our own luxury?

One the one hand, Christians, Jews, and many others have been the vanguard in welcoming strangers to our shores in the past few decades. Millions of new Americans have been resettled across our vast landscape. Yet, on the other hand, certain Christian tribes are the drivers of xenophobia and hatred, in effect repudiating the very central tenets of what it means to be a follower of God. Nothing short of the well-being of millions of suffering people is at stake here. Which path will we choose?

If you do not fully understand the compelling and nuanced story of the Hebrew Bible's accounts of sojourning people, read this book and you will learn many new things. If you believe you know that story, you, too, should read this book, as I guarantee you will learn much that you do not currently know. If your community is wrestling with how to respond to the new people from beyond our borders living in your town, read this book, too.

Finally, let me offer up a confession. I have known Mark Hamilton for decades. I do not write these words from the perch of a neutral observer. He is the epitome of what a scholar should be. He writes not only for his own particular guild of scholars. (Luckily for us, his vocational concerns are not limited to small circles of eccentric academics—my words not his). He has a passion for justice anchored in an understanding of what human communities and institutions ought to do based on an understanding of who God is and what that understanding requires of us. *Jesus, King of Strangers: What the Bible Really Says about Immigration* demonstrates a rare mastery of cutting-edge scholarship, and it renders an understanding of the biblical text that is compelling and accessible to the general reader. As such it is a work of love. As a friend and colleague, I have been the beneficiary of Mark's wisdom and knowledge for a long time now. Let me commend to you a deep dive into his wisdom and knowledge here. You will be the better for it, as I am the better for being his friend for several decades and a lucky early reader of this marvelous book.

SHAUN CASEY
Georgetown University
Armistice Day 2018

Preface

A BOOK LIKE THIS does not come about except through the encouragement of many friends and colleagues. I am grateful for the support of the members of the University Church of Christ, especially its bilingual community, for reminding me that human value transcends the laws of nations since that dignity derives from God. I also thank my editor, Trevor Thompson, for believing that this project deserved to see the light of day. My graduate assistants, Austin Holifield and Troy LaRue, read several drafts and made many astute comments that sharpened the argument. As always, my profoundest gratitude goes to my family, who sacrificed more than they should have to see this project come to pass. My wife, Samjung, and adult children, Nathan and Hannah, each commented on the work at its various stages but much more importantly encouraged me to seek sanity in a time when madness seems to prevail. Their inestimable gift of presence and love, in spite of all trials, is the greatest gift of all.

CHAPTER 1

The Reality of Migration

MOVEMENT, ALONG WITH FOOD, water, and shelter, remains
one of the constants of human existence. Our remotest ancestors apparently moved out of Africa and filled every continent
except Antarctica. The gene pools of the species flow more like riv-
ulets, intertwined and ever-moving. None of us stands still for long.

Today, of course, movement takes many forms, within and
among nations. Our fellow humans migrate for complex reasons:
pursuit of further education, hope for better jobs, and a desire to
escape war, famine, or persecution. In most cases, because leaving one's home culture poses many challenges, a migrant must
feel both a push and a pull. It becomes difficult to identify precise
motives.

For example, a few years ago the Perez family moved to my
central Texas city from Mexico after a gang kidnapped Rafael, the
father, and tried to extort protection money from his small drug-
store business.[1] Receiving no help from the local authorities, he fled
to the United States, where he had a few distant church acquain-
tances. Our diverse, though predominantly Anglo, congregation
adopted him, his wife Maria, and their two teenage daughters, Lilia

and Zoe, and helped support him while he navigated the labyrinthine process of obtaining a work visa as a religious worker. His older daughter, Lilia, finished high school and entered the university at which I teach. Rafael and Maria served alongside the rest of us, ministering to struggling people in our town, worshiping and fellowshiping with a community that tried to follow Christ's teachings about our common humanity.

At each step of the immigration process, the Perez family consulted lawyers paid for by members of our congregation. They meticulously followed the advice of their attorney at every turn.

Then the ICE (Immigration and Customs Enforcement) decree dropped on their heads. You must leave the country within days. Wrap up work, friendships, service to church members, and teaching the gospel. Go. And so Rafael, Maria, Zoe, and Lilia went. Fortunately, Lilia was able to receive a student visa in Monterey and to return to school, this time without her family. Her sister and parents still wait in Mexico. They broke no laws and contributed their labor and love to a community, and yet in the heightened enforcement of the past two years, they left. Tearful goodbyes, anger mixed with sorrow, affected us, regardless of political persuasion or background or heart language.

Soon after their departure, I was talking with a friend of mine, June, who is ninety-four years old. She grew up on a small West Texas farm, married, became a young widow raising several children, and enjoyed health robust enough for work into her early eighties. Kindhearted yet not one to mince words, she personifies for me the best of the American West with its independence, self-reliance, and compassion. "Why did they make them leave?" she asked about the departure of the Perez family, her indignation palpable. "Aren't they the kind of people we want coming here?" I thought so too. We all did.

June's question gets at the heart of much of the immigration debate in the United States and, to some extent, Western Europe. Aren't these the kinds of people we want coming here? Far from seeing immigrants as a threat, she had learned to see at least one family as a potential asset.

virtue of empathy (handwritten)

The Reality of Migration

Not everyone sees things this way, of course. American public culture has increasingly come to resemble a row among soccer hooligans in some Western European city. Hardened political positions, denigration of opponents, accusations and counteraccusations seem the order of the day. Knowledge takes a back seat to opinion. Nuance? Don't bother. Minds are made up or, rather, put on the shelf in locked boxes. The wisdom of my elderly friend seems lost.

It is hard to pin down the causes of this degradation of public discourse, but some of them are clear enough. In their study of the rise of the Tea Party, Theda Skocpol and Vanessa Williamson note both positive and negative aspects of perhaps the most visible of those movements that have included hostility to immigration among their mix of issues. As they note, in a blend of admiration and concern, "Grassroots Tea Party activism . . . marries participatory engagement and considerable learning about the workings of government with factually ungrounded beliefs about the content of policies."[2] That's academic-speak for "people know how to get what they want but don't know why they want it." The lack of empathy for vulnerable people outside our sphere of family and friends threatens the identity of our churches as explicitly Christian communities. *empathy* (handwritten)

They further observe something many of us have noticed in churches that contain large numbers of very conservative members: "Another paradox of Tea Party citizenship is the sharp bifurcation between generous, tolerant interaction within the group, and an almost total lack of empathy or sympathy for fellow Americans beyond the group."[3] This observation, heavily grounded in empirical research, expresses a paradox that Skocpol and Williamson and many of the rest of us have puzzled over.

The puzzlement certainly increased during the 2016 election season, when a large majority of white evangelicals who voted chose a man whose personal morals, style of communication, and ideas about the dignity of other human beings sit crosswise with Christianity in almost every respect. Many of us inside the church who had known of Donald Trump for years as a playboy and reality television personality were astonished that his transgressive life-style and mode of communication could find a home within the church itself. It seems impossible to square his rhetoric with the numerous statements in the New Testament about how we should communicate with each other and how we should shape our own lives. Many of us have felt betrayed by religious leaders who have justified acceptance of his policies (to the extent that his ideas of governance can be dignified with such a label) by appealing to the old shibboleths of the culture wars of the 1970s. Many of us think that a day of reckoning will have to come, and come soon.

Part of that transgressive rhetoric concerns immigration. Here the violation of basic norms of truth-telling and even decency has become commonplace. Naming immigrants as murderers and rap-ists, using the long arm of the state to crush weak people, holding the young people of DACA hostage to a misguided policy of wall building—all of these behaviors show not a strong leader but a very weak one. They do not make America great again, for they are the behavior not of a statesman but of a gangster. And yet many Amer-icans, including many Christians, accept such rhetoric as simply part of the cost of doing business.

So Skocpol and Williamson can rightly point to a breathtaking lack of respect for the facts and an equally profound lack of empa-thy for anyone outside the in-group as key factors in this politics. (In fairness, the same qualities seem to appear in parts of the Left as well.) And they are surely right to add, as those of us who love the church must acknowledge, that part of the motives of the Right has a connection to some expressions of Christianity. The survivors of the Religious Right have sometimes found a place in the mix of groups that have supported the proposed immigration "reforms."

Skocpol and Williamson wrote before the emergence of Donald Trump or the mainstreaming of the overtly racist alt-right that ac-companied his rise. The radical transgressiveness of Charlottesville had not yet appeared on the horizon. And we must take seriously their cautions against tarring people with overly broad brushes. Wanting a tax cut does not equal burning crosses. Opposition to universal, government-sponsored health insurance does not make one a sociopath. Worrying about the national debt makes sense, as the experiences of our southern European friends have shown. Yet those of us who object to both the style and substance of the attack on immigrants and many others should state clearly what we think is at stake, not least for the church's life.

In truth, this struggle to articulate alternative visions is going on all over American Christianity. While some conservative evangelicals and fundamentalists insist on fighting the culture war of the 1970s to the last ditch, a younger generation of leaders has emerged in evangelicalism to insist on both a different style and different content. They have come to doubt the idea that somehow landing a few congenial judges will radically alter the moral decision-making of large swathes of their fellow Americans. They have sickened of the political grandstanding and power-mongering that has accompanied the Religious Right's grasp at power. And they ask what any of that has to do with Jesus's announcement of a kingdom that brought sight to the blind and liberty to the captives.[4]

When Jesus spoke of that kingdom, he did not pull his ideas about it out of thin air. Rather, Jesus and the early church reporting his words and deeds resorted over and over to the older stories and poems of Israel, the texts of the Old Testament. Jesus's story was Israel's story.

Such a reality becomes clear in Jesus's description of the Last Judgment, the moment when God will resolve all the problems of human existence and make justice real. As the First Gospel relates, Jesus represented the great trial scene as an announcement of hope for the righteous and despair for the wicked, with the distinction between the two arising from the fact that the former responded properly to the royal judge. As the great ruler says, "I was hungry and you fed me, thirsty and you gave me a drink, a stranger [*xenos*] and you housed me, naked and you clothed me, sick and you nursed me, in prison and you came to me" (Matt. 25:34-36).

Jesus presents the great judge of all, himself, as the king of strangers, the ruler whose concerns extend to the most vulnerable human beings. Far from pursuing the splendors of empire and the approval of the successful, the king of all seeks the vulnerability of

example of hospitality

the prisoner, the empty stomach and shivering limbs of the poor. And he rewards those human beings who go beyond the illusions of success to the reality of human misery and the possibilities for its relief.

Conversely, the wicked neglect these acts of human kindness. Jesus's criteria for eternal salvation do not come out of nowhere. This is the point. As the king of the prisoner, the hungry, and the migrant, he simply repeats the concerns of Israel's entire history of moral reflection, as evidenced in the Bible itself.

This book reflects just such concerns. Here I hope to present a Christian viewpoint that both accurately represents Scripture's teachings about migrants and their hosts and invites non-Christians to engage in a mutually respectful moral discourse about political issues that matter. As my friend June says, "Aren't these the people we want here?"

What Do We Know?

So we should start with what we know. In their 2018 report, the United Nations and the International Organization for Migration noted that, as of 2015, about 244 million persons live in a country other than the one of their birth, making immigration a major force in today's world.[5] Many of these migrants enjoy improved prosperity, safety, and good health care in their host countries. In 2016 they sent back home $575 billion, three times the amount of formal foreign aid, in order to help families and friends.[6] This transfer of funds and knowledge elevates families, communities, and nations. At the same time, many others live outside the law and fall victim to the predations of human traffickers, dishonest employers, and corrupt officials. Indeed, the customary distinctions made for immigration—free versus unfree, laborers versus refugees, legitimate movements versus vagrancy—prove difficult to apply in concrete cases.[7]

In addition to these quarter of a billion migrants, refugees and internally displaced persons constitute a different and rapidly growing group. According to the United Nations High Commission for Refugees, the world's number of forced migrants motivated by war or governmental oppression grew from 38 million in 2000 to just under 60 million in 2014, not the sort of growth industry anyone would welcome.[8] About 22.5 million of those persons have crossed international borders, putting them into the complex systems for refugees and asylum seekers. Absent sufficient resources, most of these persons live in nearby countries, making refugee crises a regional phenomenon, in part. Less than 1 percent of such refugees permanently resettle in a new country. And since economic development, always intertwined with governmental stability, has advanced furthest in areas most distant from such catastrophic conflicts, refugees often land in many of the poorest countries in the world. The fraying of international infrastructure in an era of nationalistic competition renders the overall situation precarious at best.

The complexity and seeming hopelessness of the situation drift across our television screens or internet feeds in the videos of European coast guards rescuing sinking boats in the Mediterranean. Thanks to adventuresome journalists and the work of organizations like Doctors Without Borders, we have become more aware of the plight of Africans and Middle Easterners caught in the web of movement spun by warlords and smugglers, on one side, and the still functioning civil societies that must decide how to do good with limited resources and inadequate knowledge, on the other. Borders and the national identities they symbolize and reinforce seem increasingly airy and unreal.

However, the attempt to make them real has occupied politicians on both Left and Right since the eighteenth century, at least. Following the end of the European wars of religion in 1648, powers on that subcontinent created what is often called the Westphalian system (named for the Treaty of Westphalia ending the Thirty Years' War). In this political scheme, all states defend clearly defined borders, and everyone lives inside a state, of which he or she is a citizen. (Pirates, castaways, and itinerant billionaires offer the major exceptions to the rule.) Persons move not from village to village or

7

even province to province, but from one carefully circumscribed state to another. Since borders are ideological constructs as much as physical ones, movements across them frighten or excite those on the other side, often triggering political movements or driving populations to decide to isolate themselves, even contrary to their own rationally considered self-interest. Brexit, anyone?

Crucially, the choices *frighten* and *excite* come from the underlying conditions of the host country. Australia or Canada, for example, can welcome large-scale immigration as a percentage of their overall population in part because their vast landscapes lack people to fill them. In more densely populated regions, such as Western Europe or the United States, the backlash against immigrants, refugees, and their advocates has intensified thanks to both social pressures and the work of politicians on the make. The stories of individuals and families fade into the background before the grand narratives of nationhood, which always require a menacing "other" powerful enough to threaten but weak enough to be defeated.

In a situation so charged with structural conflict and individual opportunity, escaping the trap of binary thinking about one's own group and the "other" requires more than vague appeals to human sympathy or love. It calls for both understanding and moral clarity. We need a way of thinking about human movement that allows us to honor the best traditions of both the migrant and the host. And we need to see behind these accumulations of human wisdom the dignity of human beings as human beings. A deeper understanding of strangeness that understands migration and the reception of migrants as a vital—creative, life-giving, knowledge-producing—aspect of human existence will be required.

Alternative Narrative, Alternative Norms

For Christians, this understanding must come from our primary texts, the Bible and the creeds, and our primary practices, baptism and Eucharist. The church is the trustee of centuries of experience and thought across hundreds of cultures. Christian beliefs and practices contain within themselves resources for human flourishing. We need to exercise that trust with respect to issues of migration too.

These indispensable touchstones push the church away from a narrow construal of the issues, for at many points a Christian reflection on migration will overlap with a Jewish one since both nourish deep roots in the same texts and point to the same God. At a significant number of points, a Christian reflection will contact a Muslim one as well. So by no means do I use the word *Christian* in order to narrow the scope of this discussion to a small group or a hermetically sealed thought world.

The problem is that many Christians have lost track of the primal language of Scripture. Yes, we mount out-of-context Bible verses about God's plans for us on gilt wall hangings and hold up John 3:16 signs at football games. But the shape and flow of the Bible, its core theological ideas, and the ways it witnesses to the story of God's work in the world often become entangled with other narratives, whether that of puffed-up nationalism or uncritical celebration of the so-called free enterprise system. As Brent Strawn has recently argued, many Christians use the Bible in a garbled way.[9] Our language has become a creole, a mix of various words and grammatical structures used incorrectly. Nowhere have we more garbled the biblical language than in this matter of immigration. We must set the problem right.

When we focus on the primary texts of the Christian tradition, the Old Testament (or Hebrew Bible) and the New Testament, even when we read them in connection with the creedal statements and canonical practices that arose out of them, a proper division of labor becomes necessary. Here, then, I address a part of the whole, the Bible itself as the chief repository of the primary Christian language about God, the world, and humankind's life together. By considering the stories, poems, prayers, wise sayings, and prophetic utterances embedded in these texts, it will be possible to re-see the world of movement in which we find ourselves today.

The Church Addresses the State

How, then, can the church witness to national governments in ways that reflect the shape and flow of the Christian narrative while also finding principles for the state's moral discourse on citizenship and alienness. To be specific, the enormous scale of modern migration has raised for many countries serious questions about the proper constituency of the nation state's benefits and obligations. These debates often focus on issues of budget, law enforcement, and education, but they also go to deeper moral questions.

From the church's point of view, the principles cited for policies regarding migrants must lean toward those lying at the heart of the biblical tradition itself. If the church is to offer parts of its wisdom to the state, as all wise traditions bear an obligation to do, then what would we offer from our centuries of experiences as a body of immigrants and nonimmigrants? What could we say about the making of agreements between citizens and noncitizens in the real world?

First, although we recognize the difficulties of moving directly from the ancient text to the contemporary world, we must reject the view of some Christians for whom obedience to the state's law precludes any discussion of amnesty, accommodation to economic realities, or attention to the particulars of the suffering of immigrants. Such views should be called what they are, racism masquerading as spirituality. Christians and other persons of good will must reject the neglect of refugees and demonization of immigrants. In biblical views of law, the moral commitments behind the rules and the character of the people keeping them are crucial and subject to constant reevaluation.

Second, because of the biblical tradition's expansive understanding of humankind, the church may offer the state counsel in its debate about the character of the citizen and the alien. Over its two-thousand-year life, the church has learned the hazards of locating primary identities in political or social communities, especially those expressed in modernity as membership in a nation or citizenship in a state (two different but related concepts). Deep in our communal memory lies the experience of persecution from the Roman Empire with its pretenses to reflect the will of the divine realm, as well as civil disobedience to oppression on the part of other states. Because of this history, the church rightly entertains a deep suspicion of claims by a state to decide which of those residing within its borders fit. Baptism admits both citizens and aliens of a state to a common life that may require that, as a Christian, I disobey the immigration laws for the sake of love for the other.

Third, the church must encourage the state to explore its own moral foundations and to draw upon the best features of them to articulate policies affecting migrants. A helpful approach to this appears in, for example, six recommendations from a 2013 United Nations document on migration, which encouraged member states to "reaffirm the protection of human rights of all migrants." This commitment would take solid shape in the adoption and enforcement of international standards of protection in job markets, the elimination of human trafficking, and the discouragement of all forms of discrimination.[10] Beneath such recommendations, however, lie a set of unstated moral assumptions that the church and others of good will do well to engage.

To take the situation in the United States, for example, what would the effect of abandoning its role as asylum to immigrants and refugees be on America's self-understanding? Has not its entire history, and therefore the nature of the promises its citizens make to each other, its moral code, been underwritten in a fundamental way by the plea to the Old World to give up its "tired, poor, huddled masses yearning to breathe free." Whether a given nation has an abstract moral obligation to admit aliens is less crucial a question than whether the nature of the American moral discourse requires such admission or whether it can survive an abandonment of so fundamental a principle.

Fourth, we take a cue from the Jewish philosopher David Novak who has argued, "The main motif of biblical moral teaching is covenantal faithfulness. It is considered to be in the nature of human beings to make various covenants with each other."[11] Novak goes on to explore the work of Hugo Grotius (1583–1645), the great Christian theologian and founder of international law as a discipline, as well as the thought of the Puritans, who first worked out the connections between modern states and their inhabitants as they sought to counteract the totalitarian impulses first set forth by Thomas Hobbes. To quote Novak again: "To do better than the Puritans, biblical believers today who are committed to a democratic form of polity need a phenomenology of human agreement itself. This involves asking the most basic question: Why should I believe your commitment to me to do what you promise to do with me?"[12] At their core, the biblical tradition raises the fundamental political question of what sort of agreements human beings enter into.

Or to return to Novak's terms, what "phenomenology of human agreement" will the state employ with the persons in question? In an environment where all things are negotiable, morally committed people must focus on that question. What sort of agreement between citizens and aliens could be entered into that would protect the latter from the abuses of arbitrary deportation, subminimum wages, unsafe working conditions, poor education and health care for children, and the other realities of life for many (most?) immigrants (legal and illegal) in America and other countries today? Without a society-wide discussion of the human dimensions of immigration, it is difficult to see how a just, sustainable legal framework could emerge.

What Is to Be Done?

Today, then, the American church stands at a crossroads. Its identity is at stake. Will we succumb to the forces of extreme nationalism or remain witnesses to the good news for all? Will the honored name Christian become a gang label for one group at war with others, or will it be an invitation to all to follow the one who insisted on tangible practices by which we could learn to love our neighbor as ourselves?

This book, then, works to forestall such a crisis by identifying major landmarks on our road. This book, in fact, is a sort of emergency scholarship. I make no claim to cover all aspects of the problem with adequate subtlety and sophistication. Much like archaeological salvage operations that attempt to recover what can be recovered during a trying time, this work seeks only to aid the church's recovery of its own native language with respect to migrants. In that language, the migrants and their host find a path to a meaningful, mutually rewarding life together by pursuing shared values and practices that promote such an outcome.

Here I try to gather up various loose threads of thought—stories, rituals, poems, and prophecy—in order to make a cumulative case. No single text or cluster of texts can tell the whole tale, but together they point irresistibly to a far more open view than that which many Christians now take.

CHAPTER 2

The Bible and the Migrant

W HOSE STORY GETS TOLD, then? And why?
In a recent article, Sarah Stillman describes the research she and her team at Columbia University's Graduate School of Journalism did to document the deaths of those deported from the United States. These men and women had committed no crimes in the United States other than lacking the proper documents to stay. In case after case, she found that on returning home some people faced known, predictable dangers from gangs, former partners, or neighbors.[1]

She tells the story of Laura, arrested at a routine traffic stop in south Texas and then deported thanks to an overzealous local police officer. Laura was murdered by her ex-husband on returning home, despite her requests for help from both American and Mexican police.

And then there was Nelson, who burned to death in a Honduran prison where a local police raid had dumped him after an antigang raid. Ironically, he had fled to the United States to escape those very gangs.

And on it goes. The media headlines and the chatter of experts may focus on big structural issues or how political leaders use the

[handwritten margin note: examples of migration in bible]

stories of migrants to advance their own causes. But behind the headlines and the pontifications of talk-show pundits lie stories of real people. Suffering, resilient people.

In many ways, Stillman's ground-level perspective fits closely a biblical point of view. Key biblical stories involve movement from one culture to another: Abraham and Sarah leave Ur for a land God will show them. Moses and the Israelites stream out of Egypt, wander from desert camp to desert camp, and finally arrive in the promised land. Centuries later, their descendants, driven off by successive invasions of the great Mesopotamian empires of Assyria and Babylon, return home to rejoin their nondeported fellow Israelites in rebuilding their ancestral towns. Or many of them do, while others reside in a diaspora that still persists. In the New Testament, believers flee Rome under state persecution, while others head there to carry out their mission of spreading the good news. Not much sitting still in this text.

For centuries, then, Israelite authors paid attention to migration as they wrote many different types of texts. The drama of movement continued to fascinate. In part this fascination responded to external stimuli, the realities of forced or voluntary migrations over the mid-first millennium BCE, the time of the Old Testament's creation. Such world-historical events as wars and mass movements to and fro across the Middle East would interest creators of texts and their audiences because they affected every part of their life, from social interactions to the production of food to love and family. Yet not every stimulus comes from the outside. Intellectual traditions such as those collected in the interrelated canons of the Bible (Jewish, Samaritan, Christian) take on a life of their own as the interpretation of older texts drives the creation of newer ones. The Bible contains texts that repeatedly take up the question of the dignity of migrants and of what others owe them as fellow human beings.

These texts come back to the same ideas over and over. A key theme concerns the outsider-insider status of Israel itself. Put simply, in the Old Testament, Israel figures as both the migrating community and the host of migrants. This dual identity, in which each

[handwritten note at bottom: in group / out group]

gur = to be a migrant & not a new concept

dimension colors the other, appears again and again in the texts, shaping the reader's outlook on what it means to stand before God as a human being who both lives at home and does not.

The Israelite as Stranger

Where to begin, then? One intriguing story appears in the book of Genesis, chapter 20. Here Abraham and Sarah find themselves taking up residence as aliens in Gerar, a small state in the western Negev near the coastal plain, not far from the modern Gaza Strip.[2] As the text tells the story,

> Abraham traveled from there toward the land of the Negev, taking up residence between Qadesh and Shur, and he was a migrant in Gerar. So Abraham said that Sarah, his wife, was his sister, whereupon Abimelek, Gerar's king, took Sarah. Then God said to Abimelek in a dream one night, "You're a dead man because of the woman you took, because she is married." Since, Abimelek had not approached her, he said, "Lord, will you also kill an innocent people? Didn't he tell me, 'she's my sister' and she said, 'he's my brother'? I did this with an unsullied mind and with innocent hands [i.e., from pure motives]." (Gen. 20:1–5)[3]

In other words, Abraham pulled the same trick he did in Genesis 12, and with similar results. Here, however, the king of Gerar counters the divine threat of death with a protestation of innocence. "It's their fault," he insists.

The story is interesting on many levels. Not only does it introduce the language of migration, the Hebrew verb *gur* ("to be a migrant or sojourner"), accentuated by the pun on the place-name Gerar, but it also sets forth at least seven themes that appear repeatedly in biblical texts about migration.

1. The text begins with a person or family residing in a foreign country. Here Genesis accumulates yet another instance of

"Abraham and Sarah were here" as a way of establishing Israel's connection to the entire land of Canaan.

2. Their residency occurs in a specific place, locatable on a map, complete with its own cultural history, geography, climate, and all the accoutrements of real life. Abraham and Sarah do not reside *nowhere* but in a culture different from their own.

3. This culture has its own power structure, which the migrants rightly or wrongly perceive as menacing. Here a king takes Sarah into his harem. Like many other ancient people, he no doubt would have understood his "marriage" to Sarah as an act of alliance building, but Abraham and Sarah understood it as a way of circumventing the threats imposed on them by the power structures. The allies differed in their goals and assessments of one another.

4. Part of the menace of the host nation involves sexuality, especially the mistreatment of women. Of course, we might read this story and its companion in Genesis 12:10–20 as an instance of turning women into commodities for sale, with both Abraham and Abimelek as villains of the piece.[4] We might even read Abraham's technically correct but highly misleading "she's my sister" as a Freudian fantasy of cuckoldry, though it is more plausible to see the story as a case of the unlosable wife, an instance of the literary motif of a person or object that never goes away.[5] In its many layers, however, Genesis seems to explore yet another idea, highlighting the vulnerability of the entire migrant family, perhaps indicating that our modern reading is an instance of ethnocentrism rather than liberation.

5. The migrants devise a stratagem for survival. Sometimes the scheme works and sometimes it doesn't, but always the impulse to arrive at tomorrow prevails. Just as Jochebed put baby Moses in a basket, the midwives lied to pharaoh about the speed of Israelite births, and Esther tricked Haman and Ahasuerus, so also Abraham and Sarah find a way to hold terror at bay.

6. God takes an interest in the migrants' lives, protecting them from powerful enemies. Here God intervenes in a dream threatening Abimelek, and that communication suffices to

[handwritten: ✳ use for lesson plan]

solve the problem. Other instances, such as the confrontation with pharaoh in Exodus, require more drastic action. The difference lies in the character of the ruler.

7. Significant moral issues come into play. The story explores the agency of major characters against the backdrop of their cultures' conceptions of royal prerogatives, appropriate deal making, the communication strategies of deities, and other ideas.

This last factor seems most compelling. Storytelling in the Israelite tradition rarely resorted to easy moralizing. The biblical writers did not go into the fortune-cookie business. Rather, the stories employ the speeches and actions of the characters to explore many possible values and actions for the reader to sift and weigh. If the stories push a conclusion, they do so only at the last minute, out of respect for the reader's intelligence.

In this story, the moral values appear primarily in the interchange between God and Abimelek: God's threat to kill the king results from his taking a married woman. That is, Abimelek's attempt to carry out the culturally accepted practice of marrying a woman outside his clan after a suitable exchange of gifts, which in turn symbolized the relationship ensuing among the families and more extended social networks of both partners, rested on a fundamental misunderstanding. According to the divine judgment, Abimelek's action crossed a boundary. The crown had, perhaps unwittingly, abused a vulnerable family.

Abimelek, however, mounts his own defense (in a dream, no less). He makes several interlocking arguments that reveal his own moral commitments, or rather an alternative that the reader (and God) must consider. Abimelek seeks to exonerate himself from charges of abusing his power by emphasizing the deceptiveness of his partners in the exchange of a wife, here both Abraham and Sarah. In many legal systems, ignorance of the facts of a case can be a defense. Abimelek pleads ignorance, and God accepts the plea.

Their conversation (still in the dream!) evolves into a reflection on the transaction with Abraham as a whole: "And God said to him in the dream, 'I know in fact that you did this with an unsullied mind, so I myself prevented you from sinning against me. That's why I stopped you from touching her. So now return the man's wife, because he is a prophet and he can pray on your behalf. Stay alive! And if you don't return her, know that you will definitely die—you and all yours'" (Gen. 20:6-7). The interplay of the four characters (including the largely silent Sarah) allows the story to explore the moral dynamics of the relationship between settled and migrant persons.

Abimelek's self-defense meets divine acceptance ("I know"), and so the dream comes to seem less an announcement of doom than a warning and a call to action. Yet the rest of the conversation forecloses an easy resolution of the problem, as the text notes,

> So Abimelek got up in the morning and called all his servants and told them everything. The men were terrified. Then Abimelek summoned Abraham and asked him, "What have you done to us? What did we do wrong to you that you brought on me and my kingdom a great calamity? You've treated me in ways that just aren't done." Abimelek also said to Abraham, "What did you see/fear that made you do this thing?"
>
> Abraham replied, "I thought that there was no piety [literally, "fear of God"] in this place and that they would kill me because of my wife. Technically, she is my sister, my father's daughter but not my mother's, and also my wife. So, since God led me from my family, I have said to her, 'the way you can be loyal to me is that wherever we go, say, "he's my brother."'" (vv. 8-14)

In part, the prolonging of suspense comes from Abimelek's understandable indignation at Abraham's behavior and Abraham's odd defense. For the king, the behavior of the alien Abraham is inexplicable. His three questions, "What have you done?" "What have we done?" "What did you see?" force Abraham to defend himself. He asserts without proof that the lack of piety in Gerar (and presumably everywhere else in Canaan), a lack that would include hostility to strangers and disregard for elementary acts of hospitality such as not seizing others' wives, endangers him and thus prompts such antisocial behavior.

This defense risks rebuttal, of course, in a story in which a penitent king has just heeded the dream about a threatening deity. Indeed, Genesis hesitates to accept Abraham's argument in full, both here and in the related story in Genesis 12:10–20.[6] These texts recognize vestiges of morality in Gentile rulers. In a situation of perceived danger, Abraham apparently does not consider the possibility that his construal of Sarah's trips to foreign harems as the ultimate act of wifely loyalty might in itself pose dangers to her or himself.

So we can dismiss Abraham's reasons as self-serving at best if we want to. His assertions bump up against the text's portrayal of Abimelek as one having an "unsullied mind." Yet the story does not allow for a straight-up rejection of Abraham's claims. Abraham's arguments also sound plausible. The particularities of this theology aside, a man whose meanderings down dusty trails follow a divine command might easily find settled life, with its compromises and little acts of hypocrisy, a kind of impiety in and of itself. Foreign rulers may well steal the wives of vulnerable visitors, just as they may give free rein to genocidal thoughts. Frightened people cannot take chances. Powerful people routinely do, though usually with the lives of others. So Abraham also makes a good point.

He also questions the most powerful person in the story, God, by toying with the question of divine guidance. In a brilliant rhetorical trick, he asserts a lack of respect for deity among the Gerarites and then questions that very deity's commitment to protecting him and Sarah. He does the latter by linking his and Sarah's self-introduction as siblings to the divine call to migrate ("since God led me from my family"). He seems to say, "God must take care of me, but since this may not happen, I also have to make a plan." Part of that plan includes parlaying the legalistic parsing of relationships ("she's my sister") into a strategy fit for every foreign land ("wherever we go").[7] The dangers of migration call for such a drastic self-effacement or rather self-defense through an embrace of defenselessness.

As always, the tone of voice in this story is difficult to catch. Some readers may find Abraham's arguments amusing, though nothing in the story points to such a reading. More plausibly, his words' very outrageousness underscores the feeling of defenselessness that this migrant feels. The mix of feelings—rage, helplessness, awareness of one's own duplicity, simultaneous trust and distrust of God—almost beggars description.

Perhaps no single English word fully captures the stew of emotions. So we could be excused for borrowing a word from a different language. The Korean word *han* may describe it best. In Korean philosophy and theology, *han* denotes an unresolved bitterness against gratuitous suffering.[8] Rage at the injustice one has experienced lurks just under the surface. Letting it out can only lead to greater danger. There can be no catharsis, except in roundabout ways. Such a sustained stance toward life systemically shapes a person's approach to others, leading precisely to the sort of evaluation of the dominant culture that Abraham makes in this story. His fear and resentment (perhaps of God as well as of the local Gerarites and their Canaanite neighbors) explain the radical solution for which he opts. Whoever lives in a society in which leaders lack moral commitments must remain on guard.

At the same time, however, the divine actor offers another take on the story. Even if we do not suppose that God gets the final word in the interpretation of the story—if a final word even exists—the deity's reasoning requires attention: (1) God knew that the king's actions sprang from ignorance; (2) therefore, Abimelek received a warning rather than a death sentence; and (3) since Abraham was a prophet, here an intercessor for penitent sinners (cf. Gen. 18:16–33), a mediation should occur.

Admittedly, the third step in the divine plan of action seems asinine at first glance. Why would God command Abimelek to ask for Abraham's prayers? Given both Abimelek's and the reader's perception that Abraham's actions violate several moral limits regarding family life, gift exchange among families, intercultural relations, and probably other social norms, how can the wandering prophet be the mediator in this exchange? In part the answer lies in the role of the prophet as the Abraham story cycle conceives it, that is, as one to whom God reveals plans for destruction that require some pleading for mercy.[9] Abraham had played that role in the story of the demise of Sodom and Gomorrah, admittedly a hopeless case given the cruelty of those places. No one else *can* pray for Abimelek.

At the same time, more than formal role-play occurs here. Abraham's appeal to the deity sutures the split between the two men, just as it prevents divine intervention in the crisis to the detriment of the offending king. It also heals Abraham's own agony of soul, restoring to him agency in dealing with God and his human hosts, agency he seems to think lost.

To clarify this point, the reader must ask what God wants in this story. The aim seems to be to create a harmonious relationship between Abraham and Abimelek (and thus the Gerarites more generally) without sacrificing poor Sarah. Such a relationship in ancient societies must be cemented through the appropriate, symmetrical exchange of gifts. Such gift exchanges must be relatively transparent so as to avoid future conflict. Mutual trust trumps all else. And trust derives from experience.

Yet Abraham has disrupted such a gift exchange, foreclosed the possibility of peaceful relationships, and in fact heightened tension through his actions. The goal must now be to lower the conflict level, in part by divine intervention on behalf of the weaker party, here Abraham and Sarah.

This lowering of tension through gift giving is precisely the outcome of the story, as Abimelek returns Sarah and offers various gifts that mend the relationship with the migrant. That last move does not merely enrich Abraham. It cements ties between his and Sarah's family and their hosts.

Before turning to the story's final twist, therefore, it would be useful to think a bit more about gift exchange. In his classic study of the phenomenon, Marcel Mauss argued that the environment of gift giving is one "where obligation and liberty intermingle."[10] To be morally upright, the recipient must reciprocate in a symmetrical way. If you give me a Mercedes, I can't give you coupons to McDonald's in exchange unless I want to insult you or make an ass of myself. Thus the transfer of goods will cement a relationship, signifying the parties' present interest in amity among themselves and their promises of future cooperation.

So, the transfer of property is not a business transaction, subject to the prices of the market and purely pragmatic in intent. Nor is it a sort of lottery in which the winner takes the money and runs. Rather, it marks an end to the uncertainties of the relationship between the host and alien. The migrant enters the social network of the settled, subject to its rules and expectations, but also contributing something new to that society. By receiving a gift, Abraham acknowledges the high status of the king as one who can generously give such gifts. The migrating patriarch also acknowledges his own dependence on the king, just as he establishes his own rights to be protected by the king (and from the king). The two parties acknowledge that they owe each other something.

The anthropologist Arjun Appadurai explains the results of gift giving nicely when he talks about extreme cases of massive giving that he calls "tournaments of value." As he explains, "What is at issue in such tournaments is not just status, rank, fame, or reputation of actors, but the disposition of the central tokens of value in the society in question. Finally, though such tournaments of value occur in special times and places, their forms and outcomes are always consequential for the more mundane realities of power and value in ordinary life."[11] When ancient people gave and received gifts, they both revealed and bolstered the values they shared. Social relationships take on new life through the exchange of gifts. In the story in Genesis, these values include safety for vulnerable people, respect for legitimate authority, a willingness to listen to God (or the gods, since Abimelek was no monotheist), and various other things that most of us even today would accept with appropriate cultural adjustments.

The final surprising turn in the story comes toward the end, then. Already in the earlier conversations of the story, the narrator has hinted that Abraham's actions have brought upon Gerar various calamities other than just a royal case of guilt or fear of a deity's appearance in a dream. And so the final turn comes with the notification that "Abraham prayed to God. Then God healed Abimelek and his main wife and his secondary wives so they could give birth." Thereupon follows an editorial explanation: "For Yahweh had sterilized every womb in Abimelek's house because of Sarah, Abraham's wife" (Gen. 20:17–18).

The last part of the story brings into focus a major element of the tale, hitherto undisclosed. It turns out to be a plague story in which Abraham and Sarah pose a radical threat to their host society. The God of the Bible punishes xenophobia, which Abraham has rightly suspected in his hosts. The Gerarites' suspicion of and hostility toward migrants rebounds on itself. The feared danger from outside proves to originate within. Sterility in the king's household inevitably leads to the political instability of the entire country, but avoiding this instability requires only acceptance of the outsider as a partner.

Now, again, such an element of the story can make sense under only a couple of conditions. Hypothetically, the story might wish to portray Abraham's God as cruel, highly partial to a family of paranoid nymphomaniacs, or otherwise morally defective. However, such a reading makes no sense in the overall context of Israelite literary portrayals of suffering at the hand of foreign powers. Nor does it fit Genesis's understanding of God.

The other possibility, then, has greater face validity, namely, that the deity gives at least some credence to Abraham's fears of oppression by the various foreign rulers among whom he must live. "He is a prophet" means he is concerned with issues of justice (as in the Sodom and Gomorrah story). It also means that he must speak for God and thus must pursue truth. Both sides of this dual nature of the prophet must play a role. Since no other prophet stands in the wings ready to intervene for Abimelek, Abraham must. He must subordinate his role as the wronged husband to the higher role of third-party mediator. Abraham must embody in his own social interactions the justice that he seeks, an embodiment that can only come about through collaboration with others.

This convoluted rectangular relationship among Abraham, Sarah, Abimelek, and God makes sense if God agrees with Abraham that living in Gerar poses dangers to him and Sarah, perils that they seek to resolve (as in other stories of theirs) in an unfortunate act of sexual boundary crossing. A danger exists of the host country failing to provide goods it owes the migrants as human beings, including physical safety and a chance to support themselves. Why would an Israelite audience (or God standing in for them, as well as vice versa) find such a viewpoint plausible? Simply that such was their experience. The Lauras and Nelsons whose stories Professor Stillman tells today share a kinship with the Abrahams and Sarahs whom the Bible commemorates. The tangled episodes of their lives bear out the same themes of suffering and resilience.

Beyond Abraham and Sarah

And yet each story bears its own particularity. The literary connections of the story of Abraham, Sarah, and Abimelek are of two sorts. In the first place, Genesis 20 is the middle episode in a trio of stories about how the patriarch and matriarch attempt to manage the danger of the foreign land by pretending not to be married. They perceive the threat from the host country in sexual terms, with the wife being the object of foreign desire and both husband and wife, therefore, becoming potential victims of foreign violence, though in different ways. In all three stories (Gen. 12:10–20; 20:1–18; 26:1–11), the couple travels to a foreign land, encounters the threat especially in the person of the monarch, responds, and then finds their plan unraveling with the foreign ruler expressing consternation at their decision to circumvent sexual danger by creating it instead. Thus we are dealing with a type scene with strong folkloric elements, yet with a twist. In every case, the question of who is the hero and who the villain comes into play.[12] The texts mess with the readers' expectations, as all good storytelling does.

At the same time, the combination of the three stories in Genesis creates a new meaning. Claus Westermann undoubtedly goes too far when he sees Genesis 20 as simply an interpretation of Genesis 12 and not a story in its own right,[13] but the stories do make a certain sense in their relationship to one another that does not reside entirely in the repeated elements among them, nor in their placement in earlier sources of Genesis now combined.[14] In other words, each successive story presupposes the prior ones. This fact becomes most clear in Genesis 26:1-11, which knows of both Abimelek of Gerar and of the famine to which Abraham and Sarah responded in Genesis 12:10-20.

That is, the text explicitly connects the two prior stories of the endangered ancestors by opening with "There was a famine unparalleled since the first famine that was in the days of Abraham, so Isaac went to Abimelek the Philistine king, to Gerar" (Gen. 26:1). "The first famine" cross-references the prior story of Genesis 12:10-20 and therefore presupposes (comments on, reworks, expands) the earlier text. The reference to Abimelek brings in Genesis 20, and the combination of the three stories reminds readers that migrants repeatedly face danger.

The recall of the earlier stories does not stop there, however. The third story resolves with Abimelek commanding his people not to "touch" Isaac or Rebekah (Gen. 26:11) and threatening violators of that instruction with death. The ruler exercises the role of protector of vulnerable people and upholder of justice, just as all kings in the ancient Near East tried to present themselves. So it was before with Abraham and Sarah in Egypt and then in Gerar. In each case, the monarch as embodiment of the state must guarantee the safety of the migrant even in opposition to culture-wide hostility to them.

So this is one story told three times. Another thrice-told tale appears in Genesis 12-50, the threefold promise to Abraham (Gen. 12:1-9; 15:1-21; 17:1-27). Without exploring these rich and intriguing stories in detail, we should notice one relevant point that bears on the wife-sister stories as well. Genesis 12:1-9 famously sets up a three-sided relationship spanning time and space: the deity (Party 1) will bless Abram and his descendants (Party 2) as they interact with the nations (Party 3), leading to the blessing of those various nations as well. It is of course instructive that the interactions with those nations that follow in Genesis hardly seem blessed, at least not in a conventional, Christian pop-psychology way. Neither pharaoh nor Abimelek would have entertained warm feelings toward the Abraham family right away. And yet the realism about interethnic conflict so evident in Genesis 12–50 does not erase the promise. It merely reframes it.

The reader of Genesis comes to expect moral complexity on this and many other fronts, reflecting the untidiness of life itself. We also come to expect serious moral commitments between migrants and their hosts, including loyalty, protection from danger, and hope for the future. All these appear in the stories of blessing as well.

In pursuit of this complexity, then, Genesis offers a multilayered reading of the fate of the descendants of Abraham and Sarah, and therefore of God and God's blessing. Nothing is straightforward. Thus Genesis 15:13–14 includes in Yahweh's revelation of the future to Abraham the counsel that "you should certainly know that your offspring will be a migrant [ger, plural gerim] in a land not theirs, and they will serve them and be oppressed by them four hundred years. Moreover, I have judged the nation they will serve so that afterwards they will go out with great loot." In keeping with the stories of Genesis 12 and 20, the status of ger becomes temporary, a phase of suffering to be sure, but one leading to vindication owing to divine intervention. The story of migration ends in repatriation of goods by the suffering gerim, hence a reversal of the realities of enslavement and domination characteristic of the experience of Israel and many of its neighbors.

It is striking, then, that the promise to Abraham in the version of Genesis 17:15–16 promises to give Sarah sufficient fertility to produce an heir. Yet the focus remains on the matriarch rather than her child: "I will bless her and, moreover, give you a son from her; so I will bless her and she will become nations—kings of the peoples will be from her."[15] The promise speaks of days present and days to come, the former containing the seed of the latter. Israel talks about its identity by describing its origins as the overcoming of potential nonexistence. Life and blessing are one.

Some Preliminary Conclusions

A summary: the promise to Abraham and Sarah in Genesis 17 opens a window into an important aspect of Israel's memory of its past. That is, the tales of the patriarchs and matriarchs in Genesis 12–50 contain one of the Pentateuch's two core stories of origins. They also allude to the other, the narrative of the exodus and all the patterns of life flowing from it as the descendants of former slaves settle in a new land previously (and still) inhabited by other people. These twin stories of beginnings work together. The wanderings of a small family merge into the migrations of their far more numerous descendants, even if the stories originated separately and are imperfectly welded together even now.[16] Genesis and Exodus work together to point toward a reality that neither of them can express alone. Their juxtaposition reminds Israelite readers of their dual nature as a migratory people who becomes host of migrants and then finds itself migrating again. This two-sided story has settled deep into the self-awareness of the biblical authors.

Why did Israel insist on its status as a migratory people, even at the expense of glorification of the ancestors? Not every text goes as far as Joshua 24, which recalls the ancestors as mere pagans who inhabited Mesopotamia before trudging off to Canaan. But even Genesis, in its portrayal of all-too-human men and women, refuses to sentimentalize its past. The stories of migration unflinchingly portray the suffering and danger that people on the move experience. And even when the patriarchs and matriarchs do not conform to conventional morality, as often they do not, they carry themselves with a dignity that their descendants hearing about them can respect or even emulate. This dignity does not depend on their settledness in a land, for that sort of stability remains only a promise, always subject to the quirks of history and the morality of one generation or another. The people keep on migrating, at least in their own memories, and in those memories lie a key to their self-understanding and their view of God as their protector.

And a final point. Stories like this call into question a basic assumption that many modern critics of immigrants make, the idea

[margin note: Remind the Church of their past as migrants and host / their past as migrants]

that some people deserve benefits and others do not. As Skocpol and Williamson show in their studies of the American Right, many people subscribe to the closely related ideas that (1) government should benefit only those who "deserve" such help, and (2) it is an easy matter to identify the undeserving. The biblical stories challenge such a view because they expose a truth about us: we readily trick ourselves into believing that our obligations to one another can be negotiated without reference to the character of the parties, their relative strength and weakness, or the moral values that are not subject to negotiation. Applying consistent standards runs immediately into the subjective whims of powerful decision-makers and often excludes anyone outside the group with which the one discerning identifies.[17] We instinctively dislike moochers, but we tend to spot them in all the wrong places. And so the host society's understandable desire to protect itself from real danger easily morphs into individualized or even systemic oppression.

CHAPTER 3

Migration as Experience and Literary Theme

DANGER STARES AT EVERY MIGRANT. The story of Abraham and Sarah, though exceptional in many respects, represents a type. The Near East during the mid-first millennium saw many Abrahams and Sarahs trudging its dusty roads, alone or in groups. The Bible tells some of their stories, eventually collapsing them into its central authorizing story of the exodus, wilderness passage, and settlement in Canaan, an account of migration as a response to the terrors of oppression. The themes of the Abraham and Sarah story— residence in a foreign land with its own cultural norms and power structures that menace the stranger, especially women and other vulnerable people, the stratagems of survival that migrants employ, and divine protection from powerful enemies—play out in many biblical texts.

Those same themes also appear more widely, in altered dress, both before and during the period when the Bible came to be. Part of that larger story also needs to be told. The Hebrew Bible's characters include both Israel and its neighbors, their stories of travel for business or love of adventure, as well as for military ambition or the driving need to survive the aggressions of others. As always, the profound humanness of these experiences triggered deep theological reflection in ancient Israel and still does so today. Just as Israel subjected its older religious thoughts to the searching gaze of historical experience, so too do contemporary readers of the Bible in the church and synagogue. We find ourselves in a dialogue with other voices, fighting for our own understanding and for the well-being of others.

To be specific, we cannot understand the Bible's ideas about migration without understanding the larger discussion around those ideas, as well as the experiences that gave birth to that discussion. Israel did not initiate the discussion. Inhabitants of the ancient Near East had carried it on for centuries before. It took on a new urgency during the late period of the Israelite monarchy and the succeeding eras, when Israelites came face to face with cultures that sought to dominate them, often justifying their actions with stories and claims about the world that they had inherited from their ancestors. The following are a few snapshots of that larger discourse.

Snapshot One: Egyptian Stories of Migration

For most of its early history, Israelite culture drew heavily on Egyptian artistic customs. Indeed, Egypt had dominated the Levant (the eastern edge of the Mediterranean Sea) for much of the two millennia prior to the origins of Israel, and it maintained garrisons in Palestine until the tenth century BCE, when the pharaoh gave Gezer to Solomon as a wedding gift (1 Kings 9:15–17). Even long afterwards, Egypt remained the high-status, look-to culture for Israel and its neighbors. Goods and ideas moved across the Sinai with the people who brought them. Cultural exchange was a fact of life.

What did the Egyptians think of migration, then? Because of the accidents of survival, evidence remains incomplete. Still, alongside royal inscriptions of invasions northward into Syria-Palestine and southward into Nubia (Sudan), all involving the flight of refugees, the capturing of slaves, and the settling of Egyptian garrisons at strategic points, a few literary tales of migration have survived.

These stories reveal a discourse about the foreign lands and peoples as good in their own way, but essentially barbaric.

From the Middle Kingdom (twenty-first to eighteenth centuries BCE) comes a short story of one Sinuhe, an Egyptian official who found himself living among the Retenu, the inhabitants of Canaan. The story remained popular for many centuries, as evidenced by the fact that one late copy of it comes from the Nineteenth Dynasty (thirteenth century BCE). While no evidence of its influence on Israelites survives, the basic themes of the story would have made sense to them as well.[1]

In the tale, Sinuhe fled Egypt during a moment of political crisis, leaving an important post at court. Found by western Asian travelers whose leader he had known in Egypt, he settled with them awhile, then moved about what is today Lebanon, Israel, and Palestine before taking a job with the king of Upper Retenu. His expertise as a soldier and politician made him a useful adviser to such a ruler, who promised him, among more lucrative and tangible inducements, the opportunity to speak Egyptian to his other Egyptian consultants and hangers-on. Over time, the expatriate became almost a native, settling into a more-or-less normal life, though he never lost his love of home.

At long last, the pharaoh invited him home, noting that all misunderstandings were cleared up: "What had you done that one should act against you? You had not cursed, so that your speech would be reproved. You had not spoken against the counsel of the nobles, that your words should have been rejected."[2] Sinuhe had not committed treason, and the court of the deified ruler of Egypt had accepted his innocence, in spite of his long absence among foreigners. Or so the letter from home says. A trap or an opportunity?

Taking his life in his hands, Sinuhe finally returns home, braving an audience with the pharaoh, whose good wishes he craves but whose will always follows the needs of the state and so remains unpredictable for mere mortals, especially those long separated from the political intrigues of the palace. To his delight, Sinuhe finds that the monarch sincerely desires his return. Now he can resume his place in what he thinks of as civilization: "Years were removed from my body. I was shaved; my hair was combed. Thus was my squalor returned to the foreign land, my dress to the Sand-farers. I was clothed in fine linen; I was anointed with fine oil. I slept on a bed. I had returned the sand to those who dwell in it, the tree-oil to those who grease themselves with it."³

The text exaggerates the contrast between Egyptian comfort and Levantine misery, obviously playing up the prejudices of Sinuhe's fellow Egyptians, the readers of the tale. Yet at the same time, the story reveals both the teller's love of homeland (even with all its political pitfalls) and the sense that living abroad requires courage, not just because of the strangeness of language and customs or the physical discomforts (giving sand back to the Sand-farers and all the rest), but because of the absence of everything dear, especially the approval of those whose connections to the divine realm give meaning to human relationships. Sinuhe's time abroad interests the story's creator only as a tale of woe, not as a means of developing the hero's character in a coherent way. As John Baines has pointed out, the story resembles more the vignettes of a modern drama than "leisurely prose fiction."⁴ Readers must fill in the blanks with their own prejudices.

Anyone who has lived abroad for an extended period can recognize in Sinuhe's life a kindred spirit, even if the overblown praise of the pharaoh sounds sickeningly sycophantic. (But then, the story pitches itself as a tomb narrative, an obituary for a life well-lived, and as such would appeal to the most accepted religious tropes, hence the exaggerated language.) No matter how many successes the new life provides, the sounds and smells and sights that inscribed our earliest memories retain their allure. We always want to return home, even when we know we cannot.

The story of Sinuhe speaks of a world in which travel occurred frequently for a few people who could then tell stories of their wanderings for the entertainment and edification of others. Egyptians apparently took pleasure in such tales, for from the eleventh century BCE hails the story of Wenamun, a sassy official who travels to the Lebanese coast to buy expensive cedar lumber for use in the temple of Amun of Thebes. His skill at repartee wins the day with skeptical dwellers of the Syrian coast, who no longer fear Egypt or feel any sense of loyalty to past subordinate relationships.

Lying long in port while making deals in uncertain circumstances, surely the fate of all sailing expeditions before the advent of the steamship, requires Wenamun's patience and intelligence to win the day. His victories in diplomacy preserve his crew's life and entertain the audience of the story with a renewed sense of Egyptian intelligence, even in a world full of strangers who do not speak their language, share their customs, or fear their armies or gods. Even in a period of national political and military decline, as Egypt experienced in the eleventh and tenth centuries BCE, the story of travel in foreign lands can speak of the virtues of the homeland to which the traveler seeks eagerly to return.[5]

If stories of a fellow countryman living in a foreign land intrigued Egyptians at various times in their history, a parallel example, or rather a sort of inversion, existed in Israel as well. That was the story of Joseph, who left Canaan under duress, gained the favor of the pharaoh and his court, and thereby protected his own kinspeople. Joseph had come to power after interpreting pharaoh's dreams about an imminent famine, providing information Egyptian soothsayers could not. He commandeered the burgeoning harvests in a tax scheme that made survival possible when the harvests stopped. And he met his unsuspecting brothers as part of the customs checks at the border guarding Egypt.

In short, Joseph out-Egyptianed the Egyptians, with his special access to secret knowledge, his capacity for planning and implementing society-wide change, and his careful management of the frontiers with Asia as he spot-checked the border for dangerous intruders. The stories of Genesis 37–50 have at least general knowledge of Egyptian distrust of foreigners, a suspicion confirmed by their experiences of Asian domination early in the second millennium BCE, the period of the so-called Hyksos, and cemented in place by later domination of the entire region during the New Kingdom. The Egyptians naturally adopted the feelings of superiority that plague many dominant cultures—usually until pride leads to the complacency that prevents recognition of danger until too late.

The Joseph story speaks of one western Asian who worked his way inside the Egyptian system to benefit those whom that the system feared most. And all the while, Joseph still longed for another place, Canaan, in death if not necessarily in life.

The Joseph story helps Israelite readers question the claims of Egypt to cultural superiority while also challenging their belief that states may succeed at keeping migrants at bay. The Joseph story paves the way for the exodus, not just by explaining how the Israelites got to Egypt in the first place, but by exposing the arbitrariness of a political system that welcomes newcomers, then fears them, and then enslaves them. It is not clear that the author of the Joseph stories knew the Egyptian tales of Sinuhe or Wenamun, and in any case Genesis does not depend directly on those older works, but they all share a common interest in the migrant. The biblical story inverts the Egyptian notion that civilization found a home only in the Nile Valley, beyond which lay only barbarism and death. For Israel, the truth was the exact opposite. Egypt enjoyed a steady food supply but could also harbor fear-driven politicians, as chapter four will explore.

Snapshot Two: Beyond Egypt

Apart from the Joseph novella of Genesis 37–50, no stories quite like these appear in the Bible, though the stories of the patriarchs and matriarchs in Genesis and of Israel as a whole in Exodus and Numbers retain some elements of the travel narrative. As Yairah Amit has shown, however, the Genesis stories in particular "are not concerned with describing the journeys for their own sakes, and difficulties of the road are not discussed. The conduct of the patriarchs when their destination was reached, their developing attachment to the land, and their awareness of their new identity are the emphases of the stories."[6] In other words, the stories of Israel's ancestors contradict the Egyptian view of Canaan. No longer a hostile, uncivilized place distant from familiar gods and marked by unfamiliar customs, the land becomes a potential home, Yahweh's promised land. Not yet of course. Full arrival must wait because history does not conspire in favor of Abraham and Sarah, Isaac and Rebekah, Jacob and Rachel and Leah, or even Joseph and Aseneth.

Nor do the biblical texts naively accept another notion of the traveler common in the ancient Near East, that of the (male) hero whose adventures brought home all manner of things exotic, whether material goods or stories of derring-do. Mesopotamians at least as early as the third millennium BCE—and probably earlier, though in the absence of written texts we cannot know—told stories about such heroes.

In one of the earliest, Enmerkar, a Sumerian-speaking king of the southern city of Kish, ventured eastward on a mission of conquest. He traveled to the land of Aratta, probably in modern Iran. At the opening of the tale of Enmerkar, a spell invoking the god Nudimmud sets the story during the time when all human beings spoke the same language in addressing the gods and had only recently innovated warfare as politics by other means. Utopia had only recently met its demise. The tale remains obscure, brief, and perhaps less exciting to us than to its first hearers, but it does reveal the allure of foreign travel as a royal enterprise. The traveling hero took the stage of people's imagination very early on.

Not so obscure to us, or the ancients, is the tale of Enmerkar's successor Gilgamesh, a real king of the early third millennium BCE around whom many legends arose and whose travels and conquests grew into one of the foundational epics of Mesopotamian culture. This hero and his friend Enkidu took off on a road trip that brought them into battle with monsters and into conversation with the survivor of the great flood. Along the way, they proved their manhood through impossible feats of strength and courage. The stories of Gilgamesh developed over a period of more than a millennium and by the time of Israel's arrival on the scene had become foundational for several cultures in the region.[7]

During the first millennium, long after the formation of the Gilgamesh Epic and its spread throughout the Near East, the kings of Assyria modeled themselves on the ancient hero, drawing on its themes as they presented their military campaigns as heroic adventures motivated by piety as well as the desire of accruing fame and glory for themselves and their nation.[8]

Given the influence of the Gilgamesh stories on later stories, up to and including the *Thousand and One Nights* of Scheherazade, it should not be surprising that the Bible alludes to Gilgamesh at least obliquely. For example, Ecclesiastes 4:12's "three-stranded cord cannot be quickly undone" quotes a proverb also cited in *Gilgamesh*, while the call to "seize the day" in Ecclesiastes 9:7-9 parallels the advice of Shiduri the barkeep in the older story as well.[9]

More generally, the hero story finds biblical parallels in the adventures of Samson and Saul, Israelite heroes whose flaws of character, overconfidence and impatience, canceled out their physical prowess. Yet there the parallels reveal an important difference: whereas the Mesopotamian tales admire the hero (even while fearing him), the biblical narratives do not. In Israel's stories, the famous men—and they are all men—fall victim to their own lack of self-control. Their self-inflicted failures expose the ultimate absurdity of the idea of the heroic traveler. Israelite writers cannot stomach the uncritical merger of power and virtue, preferring instead either to lampoon the great heroes or make them over into tragic figures.

In short, the parallels between Israel and its neighbors exist, but with a twist. The traveler who gains fame by cutting down trees in Lebanon or slaying giants or spurning goddesses, all themes from the Gilgamesh tradition that made their way into first-millennium political propaganda, falls by the wayside. The traveling hero does not impress. Not that Israel simply wants to stay home. Rather, the fame and glory bit comes at a cost that the Israelite religious tradition does not wish to pay.

Snapshot Three: Alienness and Forced Migration

The payment comes in another form. Yet another dynamic of alienness comes to Israel's consciousness from the outside, borne not so much by literary artifice as by sword and fire. Beginning in the 730s BCE, the emergent Assyrian Empire began a practice of sustained deportations of subject populations in more recalcitrant parts of their empire. The policy worked as part of a repertoire of options, including tribute collection, replacement of local rulers with more pliant relatives or nonroyals, destruction of cities and surrounding farmland, and, as a last resort, the complete annihilation of an area's population. Solid statistics do not exist from the century of Assyrian rule, but the numbers of dead or deported ran to double-digit percentages of the overall population, disrupting centuries-old cultural patterns and stimulating religious and artistic responses. Today's carnage in Syria would have seemed familiar to Assyrians and their neighbors.

The Assyrians did not perfect state terror, an art still progressing, alas. But their ancient precursor of the Trail of Tears triggered reflections from the various parties, most notably the Israelites.

In defense of the destruction, the Assyrian emperors from Tiglath-pileser III (745–727 BCE) to Assurbanipal (669/8–627 BCE) all left multiple inscriptions, usually accompanied by highly graphic reliefs commemorating their military campaigns and the consequent creation of refugees and deportees. Many of these inscriptions graced the royal palaces of the various Assyrian capitals, though others appeared in the conquered cities and at crossroads of major highways. Even for the mostly illiterate subjects of these rulers, the very presence of the monument, much less the pictures gracing it, bespoke Assyrian power and the ever-present threat of forced migration. The monuments reminded everyone that forced movement could always occur unless everyone played nice with their overlords.

While the various rulers could describe their actions differently, a few typical examples give a sense of the whole. Accordingly, Tiglath-pileser III had inscribed in his royal palace at Kalḫu such texts as "I captured (and) defeated the cities . . . Ḫista, Ḫarabisinna, Barbaz, (and) Tasa, as far as the Uluruš River. I carried off 8,650 people . . . horses, 300 mules, 660 asses, 1,350 oxen, and 19,000 sheep."[10] He continues that he had resettled at the destroyed sites a new population deported from elsewhere in his empire. The numbers and names change, but the message remains the same: deportation was an instrument of imperial administration for which neither Assyria nor its successor state, the Neo-Babylonian Empire, felt any need to apologize.

Nor did all the client kings of the empire. For example, the rulers of the small kingdom of Samal (modern Zençirli in southeastern Turkey) left behind a series of inscriptions in which they commemorated their ability to find a role in the Assyrian Empire as beneficiaries of its policies, including deportation. The earliest of these rulers, the ninth-century king Kilamuwa, mentions that he asked for Assyrian help when his enemies threatened to overwhelm him (much like Ahaz of Judah almost a century later). Assyrian intervention allowed him to "be like a father and a mother" to his subjects and give them various gifts from the booty he had acquired in war.[11] Decades later, his successor Bir-rakib boasted of his ties to Tiglath-pileser III, which allowed him to make his subjects "masters of silver and masters of gold."[12] That is, the king could redistribute the spoils of war among his people. So empire and the appropriation of goods and people benefited some. At least political speech claimed as much.

In contrast to these top-down views of imperial "heroism" justifying the suffering of other people, the biblical texts present the experience of deportation, of forced migration in a different light. For example, the book of Isaiah contains oracles that reflect on the mass deportations of the eighth and sixth centuries. Among the earliest oracles, Isaiah 10:5–18 addresses Assyria as the "staff" that Yahweh uses in anger to smash Israel and Judah. For the prophet, Yahweh uses the Assyrians' innate desire to "annihilate . . . to cut off nations, not a few" (v. 7) to make the Israelite lands into a "ruin like the dust outside" (v. 6). The Assyrians think of themselves as the ruler of rulers ("aren't my nobles kings in every case?" [v. 8]),[13] and the Israelite capitals of Samaria and Jerusalem as just new stops in the long line of sacked cities making up their empire. Isaiah sees more deeply into history, however. He takes a longer view. That is, the prophet recognizes that different players can interpret the same events differently. For him and his few appreciative readers—the

39

majority of his audience being of the unappreciative sort, as Isaiah 6:9-10 makes clear—the deportations made sense as actions of an appropriately angry deity seeking to eliminate political cruelty within Israel by subjecting it to political cruelty from without. Yet Isaiah also recognized that for Assyria the destruction followed its own logic.

A century later, the prophet Nahum described the demise of Nineveh, the final capital of the Assyrian Empire. In graphic terms, Nahum detailed the chaos of the final moments of the city as its defenders rushed about trying to stave off disaster (Nah. 2:1-11 [English 1:15-2:10]). Power failed in the end as implacable justice prevailed.

A bit later in the book, the reasons for Assyria's demise become clearer as the prophetic speech sets that event in a larger historical context. The short collection of oracles includes the pertinent verse

> Also, she [Thebes] is for deportation, she goes into exile.
> Yes, her babes are smashed at the intersections of all the streets;
> they cast lots for her somebodies and all her big shots are bound
> in fetters (Nah. 3:10).[14]

Now what had happened in Egypt fifty years earlier, when the ancient Egyptian capital fell to Assyrian armies, would happen in Assyria. For Nahum, the end of the Assyrian Empire marks a moment of poetic justice, in which the deporter becomes the deported, the humiliator the humiliated.

Snapshot Four: *Golah* as a New Reality

To speak of this turn of the screw, Nahum picks up a bit of vocabulary that seems to have come into its own during the late seventh or early sixth century BCE, the Hebrew noun *golah*. This noun sometimes denotes the state of being deported from a homeland to a new location, and sometimes the group so deported. It begins to show up more frequently in texts at the transition from Assyrian to Babylonian rule, probably not because of a new phenomenon of mass deportation and refugees but because the continued existence of displaced communities and communication between them and their homeland required new terminology, along with new stories and songs to use it.

This new word *golah* described a new reality for the eighth to sixth centuries BCE, mass forced migration and the subsequent creation of communities of Israelites and others living outside their ancestral homeland. English translations at least since the sixteenth-century Geneva Bible have often rendered the Hebrew word as "captivity" (so KJV, ASV, NRSV) or sometimes "exile" (NEB, JPS Tanakh), though in truth neither gloss quite captures the meaning. The deportees did not clank about in chains or rot in jail cells, nor were their movements necessarily restricted in the new lands of their settlement (as the movements of the prophet Ezekiel back and forth indicate). *Exile* improves on *captivity*, but even so, *exile* implies both a desire to go home eventually (a longing that Jews even today wrestle with) and a legal structure making that return difficult, as well as a group consciousness of solidarity in living far away. Not always did such a reality exist.

So perhaps it is better to leave *golah* untranslated for the moment, preferring instead to map its occurrences in biblical texts. The earliest appears to be Amos 1:15, from the eighth century, which describes the king of the Ammonites, Israel's neighbors to the northeast, going into *golah*, that is, being deported by the Assyrian rulers. Jeremiah 49:3 quotes this line (with slight modifications) a little over a century later. Between these two prophets, Nahum uses the term, as already indicated.

Most usages refer, however, either to the Babylonian deportations of the early sixth century or to the resulting community residing away from the land of Israel. So 2 Kings 24:15–16 reports that "He deported [*way-yegel*] Jehoiakin to Babylon along with the queenmother, the king's wives, his courtiers, the landed nobility. He led them up as a *golah* from Jerusalem to Babylon. (In addition, there were) all the mighty warriors (7,000), artisans and metallurgists (1,000), all the people capable of war making. And Babylon's

JESUS, KING OF STRANGERS

king brought them as a *golah* to Babylon." That is, Nebuchadnezzar lopped off the top of Judahite society in order to make resistance to his overlordship impossible. The term *golah* does not seem yet to designate a coherent group except in the estimate of the conqueror. It is not yet a self-defined, self-contained community, but rather an assemblage designed to prevent true community from forming.

But notice the language of movement in 2 Kings 24. The nobles and technicians of Judah move *from* Jerusalem *to* Babylon. Aside from the slight appendix ending the book in 2 Kings 25:27-30, a note about Jehoiakin's status in Babylon as a sort of hostage for his people's good behavior, neither 2 Kings nor the Deuteronomistic History of which it is a part expresses any interest in what happens in Babylon. Removal of people is the thing.

It is ironic, therefore, that what Nebuchadnezzar sought to prevent occurred anyway. His handpicked ruler, Zedekiah, revolted. More importantly, a group consciousness survived the deportations. Accordingly, the book of Jeremiah could speak of a cohesive *golah* community,[15] while the roughly contemporary book of Ezekiel shifts the emphasis slightly from the people to their location in Mesopotamia.[16] Moreover, while one may exaggerate the cohesiveness of the descendants of these deportees as they returned to the ancestral homeland after the collapse of the Babylonian Empire (as well as their level of loyalty to the successor state, Persia), at least some element of Israelite life survived the Babylonian (and earlier, Assyrian) depredations precisely because their deportation forced them to rethink their customs and the theology underwriting them. So by the time the book of Ezra uses the term *golah* for events in the fifth century BCE, it has come to denote a group that has returned *from* Babylon *to* the environs of Jerusalem. These "children of *golah*"—literally the descendants of deportees—must work out a new identity free from idolatry and centered on the temple (which their immediate ancestors could only remember through their tears).[17] Part of that identity involved the search for clarity about their relationship to foreigners.

This small foray into vocabulary, then, reveals not just that human catastrophes require new language, even if the neologism uses preexisting vocabulary as its base. As a result of the terrible experiences of their encounters with more powerful nations, Israel grew in their awareness of what it meant to be a stranger in a strange land. We also see that the language denotes a way in which human beings interact with their oppressors, their own and others' lands, and their own past. *Golah* evokes a set of associations. It furnishes a seedbed for metaphor, and if for metaphor, then for human reflection.

Beyond the Album: Toward a Theology of Outsideness

Where does the reflection lead? When the biblical texts think of Israel's experiences of movement, they recognize the range of motivations of both those moving and those forcing them to move. They also acknowledge that the horrors of forced migration know no ethnic boundaries since Israel shares the experience of being in *golah* with the Egyptians (Jer. 46:19) and Ammonites (Amos 1:15; Jer. 48:7; 49:3), as well as many others. Conquering armies do not apply theological tests to their victims as a general rule.

Perhaps more shockingly, at least some biblical texts can question even the uniqueness of Israel's foundational story of movement as a moment of salvation, as Amos 9:7 does when it asks,

Aren't you like the Cushites to me, Israel's children? (This is) Yahweh's oracle.

Didn't I bring Israel up from Egypt's land, and the Philistines from Caphtor [the Aegean region] and Aram from Qir [Anatolia]?

Many people migrate, and in that movement resides the possibility of dignity and meaning-making. Yahweh can exercise mercy or discipline, as needed, in the movements of many peoples, not just Israel. Admittedly, the book of Amos ends by recognizing that Israel's migration story differs in important ways from others, and yet Israel's God may offer protection and deliverance to others on the move.

At this point, then, an important piece of Israel's understanding of migration becomes a little clearer. Migration, whether voluntary or involuntary or somehow both, offers an opportunity for learning by all the parties involved. Human beings must not allow the suffering of others or their own suffering to induce stupefaction. We must think.

Amos's contemporary Hosea makes this point as well. Hosea 11 comes at a strategic position in that prophetic book, which follows a three-part structure (chaps. 1-3, 4-11, 12-14), each of which hammers out a litany of social critique but turns at the end to words of hope. Hosea 11 offers the longest of three words of hope, but not before throwing up its hands at Israel's stubborn refusal to live into its own story and highest values. The pivotal moment comes with a reflection on the realities of forced migration: "he [Israel] returns to Egypt's land, and Assyria is his king" (Hos. 11:4). That is, in Hosea's lifetime the Assyrian Empire annexed the northern Israelite kingdom, prompting some of its citizens to flee south to Egypt, where they could find refuge, and others to resettle involuntarily in the Assyrian Empire itself (cf. 2 Kings 17:5-6). For the book of Hosea, this tragedy of deportation prompted an educational moment for two of the book's major stakeholders: for Yahweh, who cannot in the end abandon the beloved people, and for the readers of the book, who must decide ultimately whether they wish to embrace wisdom (Hos. 14:10 [English 14:9]).

Hosea 11 and the book more generally say many important things about human nature, the discussion of which would take us far afield. For now, it is interesting to think about how the church has read this text over the centuries, and how that reading might inform contemporary deliberations. An instructive example—and one must suffice, alas—comes from the great fifth-century commentator Cyril of Alexandria. In the 420s, Cyril wrote a commentary on the Minor Prophets. His remarks on Hosea 11:4 capture the pedagogical dimensions of the text well:

> On leaving his homeland, the text says, in fact, Ephraim in his depravity made Egypt his own country, as it were, out of fear of

the misfortunes of war. But he became subject to Assur himself and bent his neck to a foreign ruler, being reduced to such a point of hardship. . . . Though God offered an amnesty, in fact, and, as it were, bade them reform and return to his will by abandoning depravity and rising up from the depths of idolatry, they culpably ignored him and *were not willing to return*.[18]

Cyril picks up Hosea's emphasis on Israel's culpability in its deportations, but he thinks that his own readers must learn from the mistakes of the ancestors. That is the crucial point. Migration is a form of education, even in the extreme case when the community experiencing it understands it as divine punishment.

Cyril's uncompromising view loses track of much of the subtlety of the biblical texts themselves, however. For the prophetic books, forced migration educated Israel because it allowed them to escape the temptations of idolatry and social injustice. By experiencing the tragedies of war and its aftermath, Israel could come to treasure the virtues of peace. By experiencing the state violence as it disrupted cultural norms, shattered families, and erased the memories of place and ancestors, Israel could write texts that treasured those valuable things now lost. And by recovering memories and practices and ultimately their own land, Israel could properly value the experience of migration as a vehicle for divine mercy in spite of all appearances to the contrary. The contours of that appreciation deserve a closer look.

CHAPTER 4

Exodus and Exile

C YRIL'S READING OF HOSEA'S interpretation of forced migration
provides an important clue to the overall picture: for a community to survive, it must wrestle with its experiences and find
meaning in them. Taking responsibility for history poses many serious challenges, as Israel's prophets and sages acknowledged. Even
if that meaning involves radical self-criticism, the alternative of
meaninglessness leads only to the abyss. Just as today we show our
abhorrence of meaninglessness by resorting to historical, scientific,
sociological, psychological, or other modern explanations of causes
and effects, so too do these Israelite texts seek an even deeper explanation, a religious one. The quest for an explanation comes from a
deep place in our psyche.

Yet the prophetic acceptance of blame—"we experience deportation because God justly punishes our sins"—does not sum up the
entirety of Israel's approach to the problem. Rather, this mature,
morally courageous act of responsibility-taking intermeshes with
other lines of thought, including the critique of God's failure to
temper history so as to protect the innocent. Those concerns appear in Lamentations or Job, for example. More importantly, the

prophetic critique coexists in the biblical canon with a larger narrative of exodus and exile in which the repeated deportations, though spanning three or four generations, nevertheless make up only an episode in a longer story of election and redemption. Cyril's interpretation of exile as an opportunity for education, or moral therapy so to speak, turns out to be an appropriate reading of the more ancient Scriptures that he inherited.

The prophets, then, often conceived of forced deportation as both divine judgment on sin and a last chance for rehabilitation. This two-sided nature of a historical tragedy made sense to them because they knew another drama of redemption in which the suffering of people was featured. That larger story bears the name of the exodus, the time when Israel migrated as a response to oppression. The memory of the exodus created a framework for understanding the deportations of later centuries. Exodus and exile merged in the collective consciousness of at least some of the biblical writers. Exploring how this merger occurred reveals important aspects of the Bible's understandings of the life of Israel as both migratory host and host of migrants.

Exodus as Israel's Paradigmatic Memory

To understand how Israel's conception of the exodus shaped its understanding of itself in relationship to migrants and migration, we might begin with a few general observations about human groups and how they handle collective memory. First, all cultures tell stories about their origins. One thinks of America's love-hate relationship with the Founding Fathers, or the British emphasis on "1066 and all that," or the countless monuments to past heroes (or villains, depending on one's lights) that grace city squares around the world, or even the cities or regions named for those same heroes, St. Petersburg, Washington, Santiago, Alexandria, Lusaka, to name a few. Few things are more characteristically human than our drive to make sense of the world by retracing our steps and debating their significance. So also Israel referred to its own past as a model, positive or negative, for ongoing action.

Second, memory as a human phenomenon presents itself to us in very complicated ways. Even as an individual, I remember all sorts of things, some without trying, some with a small effort, some only after much toil and sweat. Often I remember things against my will, deeds of mine I wish to consign to oblivion but cannot. And I may misremember, conflating events or placing the wrong people in them or fouling up their temporal relationship to other events. Memory tricks us, as every fan of courtroom dramas knows.

This complexity multiplies when the mind remembering bears a collective name, and yet labels such as shared, collective, or interpsychic memory also fit our experience as social beings. We remember together, and this memory, too, may come to us unbidden or in opposition to our desires, as well as through the careful cultivation of practices of commemoration.

All of these observations apply to Israel's memory of the exodus. When, how, and even whether the exodus occurred has prompted many historical studies of varying methods and conclusions, some more useful than others.[1] For present purposes, there is no need to revisit that discussion, though I do think that Israel's consciousness of having originated outside their own land calls into question the excessive skepticism of some historical reconstructions.[2] Something happened that catalyzed Israel's emergence as a new people independent of Egyptian domination, self-aware of its own difference, and committed to a new engagement with Yahweh. In addition, the community that resulted from that primordial event continued to meditate on it as a touchstone for moral and religious self-examination.

In short, by constantly retelling the exodus story, Israel found direction for the future. The drama's characters and their dilemmas lived on: Moses and Aaron, pharaoh and Yahweh, anonymous slaves and their equally anonymous taskmasters. Midwives and mothers popping out babies. Soldiers and suffering people. And always the story leans forward toward the day when the people will move, their migration necessitated by the impulse of freedom.[3]

The exodus story figures in many parts of the biblical canon, the book of Exodus in the first instance, then the rest of the Pentateuch (especially Leviticus–Deuteronomy), and finally many shorter references scattered throughout prophetic, narrative, and liturgical texts. The story in its various permutations became the presupposition of Israel's self-understanding, the one agreed-upon event whose significance, if not precise meaning, lay beyond dispute.

Exodus and Exile: A Convergence

This same story merged into the story of exile, as well. The migration long ago from Egypt assumed a complex relationship to the more recent migrations of the eighth to sixth centuries BCE. Sometimes Israelites saw the relationship as one of opposites, with the Assyrian and Babylonian mass deportations undoing the exodus, calling into question the older story as Yahweh's promissory note to Israel. Other biblical texts assume a more complex relationship between the two stories, making them not so much opposites as two events of a kind. In other words, Israelite theologians kept on thinking about the two historical moments as windows into human nature. They recognized that communities often move in response to the cruelest human passions. The merger of exodus and exile could describe two sides of a much wider pattern of human behavior and experience.

Amos

Apparently that merger dates to the period of the monarchy, the era of the initial deportations themselves. For example, probably the earliest text blurring the chronological gap between exodus and exile appears in Amos 2:9-10, part of a longer critique of the abuse of poor Israelites by their wealthier neighbors. After scoring the rich for "selling the righteous for silver, the impoverished for a pair of shoes" (Amos 2:6) and using poor women as sexual objects ("prostitute" being too dignified a title, perhaps), the prophet signals his, or rather God's, shock at their behavior by noting that

> I destroyed the Amorites in front of them,
> who was as tall as cedars, as lofty as oaks.
> Yes, I destroyed their fruit on top and roots below
> and raised you up from Egypt's land,
> brought you through the wilderness for forty years
> to inherit the Amorites' land. (2:9-10)

The oracle against Israel, part of Amos 1-2's drumbeat of complaints against every nation in the environs culminating in his own people, concludes with a description of a people defeated in war and fleeing for its life (Amos 2:13-16). Amos captures the chaos accompanying the destruction of the northern kingdom with all the tragic movements of deportees and refugees following in its train.

The linkage between exodus and exile here, obvious on the surface of the text, nevertheless remains a bit oblique. The prophet does not fill in all the details of the argument, preferring that the one hearing the oracle decide on its import. He expects the audience to know the story of their ancestors' triumph over the aboriginal population of Canaan, the Amorites. But the moral argument goes unspecified. Does Amos assert that

1. since Yahweh saved all of Israel from oppression, Israel should not play themselves off against each other (an argument for group solidarity);
2. oppression of the vulnerable should be "foreign" to Israel, more characteristic of an empire like Egypt than of the people of Yahweh (an argument for ideological purity);
3. the displacement of the Amorites shows the ultimate end of oppressive people, a warning to which Israel should take heed (an argument from the general shape of human history); or perhaps
4. Yahweh's willingness to dislocate peoples depends on their be-

havior, not some preexisting relationship since election does not give Israel a free pass (an argument from theology proper)?

Perhaps Amos intends all these things. Since the book does not explicitly lay out every step in the argument and does not overtly claim that the pre-Israelite population sinned in a uniquely heinous way,[4] we should be content to say that for Amos, Israel has failed to live out the implications of the exodus for itself.

Something about their experience of migration, though centuries in their past, should have led them to greater empathy for each other in the present. It did not.

That it did not requires further reflection, as well as more explicit detailing of the relationship between the exodus story and Israel's moral commitments. Amos diagnoses a disease of memory in his hearers, forgetfulness in the service of self-justification. Other texts in Israel's Scriptures seek to cure that malady.

Psalms

One approach appears in the book of Psalms, which includes several poems inviting a congregation of worshipers to rehearse the key events of the exodus in order to remind themselves of their core identity (Pss. 77; 105; 106).

Perhaps the most instructive of them, Psalm 78, opens with a call to the hearer to

> Listen, my people to my instruction;
> > turn your ears to my mouth's words.
> I will open my mouth with a proverb,
> > articulate ancient puzzles. (Ps. 78:1-2)

The ancient puzzles in fact repeat the same story: God rescued Israel from Egypt and succeeding hard patches of oppression, while Israel responded to the saving acts of God with idolatry and other acts of ingratitude.

The climactic moment comes near the end of the poem in verses 56–68, which merges two moments of time:

> Yet they tested and infuriated God Most High, not observing his advice.
> Disloyal and faithless like their ancestors, they tangled up like a defective bow.
> They annoyed God at their open-air sanctuaries, irritated God with their idols.
> God heard and disposed of them, completely rejecting Israel,
>> abandoned the temple of Shiloh (the tent where he dwelt with humanity),
>> gave his power to deportation, his crown to enemy control,
>> bludgeoned his people by the sword, disposed of his inheritance.
> Fire devoured his young men, not sparing his young women.
> His priests fell to the sword, but his widows did not weep.
> The Lord roused from sleep, like a guy dazed with wine,
>> struck his enemies on every side, giving them permanent shame,
>> and rejected the tent of Joseph, deselecting the tribe of Ephraim
>> yet selecting the tribe of Judah, Mount Zion, which he loved.

The lines skip three centuries or so, from the eleventh-century BCE destruction of Shiloh by the Philistines to the demise of the northern kingdom (here called Joseph and Ephraim) in the late eighth century. They also comment on the end of the northern kingdom of Israel as a vote of confidence in its southern neighbor, Judah, a view that Jeremiah comes to question when revisiting the same story of Shiloh's tragic fate (Jer. 7:12) and the authors of 2 Kings also ultimately reject as insufficiently critical of southern behavior (2 Kings 17:19–20). Psalm 78 thus seems to date to the period between the first invasions by the Assyrians and the final ones by the Babylonians, when the moral superiority of Judah seemed plausible, at least to some people.[5]

More importantly, Psalm 78 provides the linkage missing in Amos by asserting that the contrast between divine mercy and human intransigence goes back to the beginning of Israel's history. The story of the exodus implies the story of sin as well, Egypt's and Israel's. And most to the point, the story of migration goes two ways, both from a place of oppression to one of freedom and in the opposite direction. Physical movement need not correlate with moral disposition directly, and the past cannot predict the future. The slave may leave Egypt without Egypt leaving the slave.

Psalm 78 exposes, then, a problem with Israel's uncritical telling of the exodus story as one of misunderstanding and misrepresentation. When Israelites fail to report their ancestors' catastrophic decisions or seek to hide the mistakes of the storyteller's own generation, the story begins to deviate from a truthful representation of the larger patterns of history. Nostalgia has no place in the psalm's recounting of the ancient story. Israel cannot be made great again, because it never was great.

Deportation and destruction, the psalm insists, have occurred repeatedly because Israel's sins did as well. In this case, therefore, responsibility-taking shows the moral courage of the creators and users of the psalm as they attempt to make sense of history as a rolling tragedy. The psalm hopes, however, that the past may no longer predict the future since God has chosen Zion as a place at which Israel may yet find a good life under its divine overlord.

That hope proved illusory, however. Judah fared no better at the end than had its northern neighbor since the deportations came south with the Babylonians.

This latter series of events, the invasions of the entire region by Nebuchadnezzar in 605–604, 597, and 587–586 BCE, affected the creation of the literature that became the Bible more than any other single event. It would be hard to overestimate the importance of the Babylonian incursions on all subsequent history. In many senses, Jews and Christians still deal with the implications of that historical moment.

History Writing

Among their lasting legacies, the incidents of the early sixth century cemented together the older exodus story and the forced migrations that had begun almost a century before Nebuchadnezzar's predations. These seemingly disconnected events became scenes in a consistent drama.

Important signposts in that story appear in the recounting of the destructions of the two Israelite kingdoms, which appears in 2 Kings 17 and 25. These two texts sum up a long historical case that the longer work in which they appear, which modern scholars call the Deuteronomistic History (Joshua–2 Kings), builds by both reporting earlier attempts to link exodus, temple, and kingship (1 Kings 8:12–21) and showing at length the instability of that triangle of intermingled sacred and profane behaviors. The writers of Israel's first full-scale history do not find within the stories they record or the characters they so brilliantly portray any basis for confidence in human nature.

First Kings does try to find such confidence in Yahweh's mercy, however. For example, 1 Kings 8:46–53 contains one of a series of entreaties that the text attributes to Solomon at the dedication of the Jerusalem temple. The petition foreshadows the migrations that come at the end of the book:

> When they [the Israelite people] sin against you—since there is no human who doesn't sin—and you are angry with them and hand them over to the enemy and deport their deportees to the enemy's land, whether far away or near, and then they repent in the land to which you deported them, repenting and petitioning you in the land of their deportation, admitting that "we have sinned, erred, and done evil," sincerely repenting in the land of their enemies who deported them and praying to you in the manner of their land which you gave to their ancestors, the city that you chose and the temple that you built for your name, please listen in heaven your abode to their prayer and petition and defend them. Please forgive your people who sinned against you of all

54

their errors that they erred with respect to you, give them mercy before their deporters, and have compassion on them. Because they are your people and your possession that you brought from Egypt, from the midst of an iron crucible. (vv. 46–50)

In the typical convoluted style of Deuteronomy and texts influenced by it, the prayer utters seeming asides that make the chief point ("there is no human who doesn't sin," "because they are your people"). Israel's sins come out of human nature and should surprise neither the human wrongdoers nor their divine patron. According to the prayer, Yahweh should anticipate sin and therefore should provide for deliverance from it even after the forced migrations that the people experience. Building a temple, no matter how grand or carefully run, will neither forestall the suffering nor counteract imperialist aggression of the type that the Assyrian and Babylonian states brought to a high state of art.

Perhaps the most astonishing line in this cheeky, almost brazen prayer comes near its end: "because these are your people." The exodus migration becomes here not so much a moral litmus test for Israel as one for God. Yahweh must restore the deported, brutalized people because history knows the earlier event of just such a restoration. True, the prayer shows no confidence in the human capacity to avoid catastrophe, but retains a hope that the suffering arising from the various deportations that terminated the two Israelite kingdoms could lead to the kind of self-examination that makes change possible. By acknowledging the near inescapability of human error, the prayer puts the responsibility for human well-being squarely with God.

Isaiah 40–55

The crisis of confidence visible in different forms in these texts, perhaps inevitable during periods of great suffering, led at least some Israelite theologians to rethink the relationship between exile and exodus in yet another way. They opted for a new exodus that would reverse the suffering of exile by bringing the deportees back to their native land, not simply to resume their old ways but rather to reform them and thus to live into the meaning of the exodus as these thinkers saw it. Perhaps the most significant exposition of such a view appears in Isaiah 40-55.

To take a few examples, Isaiah 43:16-19 employs exodus language to describe the return of the refugees to the homeland:

> Thus says Yahweh, the one setting a path through the sea,
> a trail through the mighty waters,
> the one sending forth chariot and horse, warrior and strong man
>   together.
> They lie, not getting up, extinguished like a wick, quenched.
> You don't remember the past nor consider bygone things.
> Truly, I am doing something new—now something previously
>   unknown emerges.
> Yes, I am making a way through the desert, rivers in a wasteland.

The "something new," the return of the deportees, surpasses the exodus in dramatic importance (though it has found no Cecil B. DeMille to bring it to the silver screen). Yet the prophet borrows the old language of the exodus ("path through the sea," "chariot and horse" evoking the events of Exodus 14-15) because that imagery both offered the most dramatic images of positive change and articulated a truth about the nature of Israel as a people needing rescue from foreign tyranny. The migrant became the model human being, as it were, rather than merely the guilty paying the price for sin. Isaiah 40-55 moves away from other prophetic speech by opening with the announcement that the people have "paid fully for all their sins" (Isa. 40:2). The migrants' suffering takes on greater significance.

Isaiah 40-55, often called the Second Isaiah and usually understood to date to the latter part of the sixth century BCE, when the Persian Empire absorbed the predecessor state of Babylonia, repeatedly speaks of a new exodus. The descendants of those deported by Nebuchadnezzar will resume their place in the Israelite homeland, where they will worship the one God and live together in ethical ways. While other prophetic texts that speak of a return leave the exodus connection to one side while also believing that the return of the refugees would mark a revival of former prosperity (e.g., Jer. 31:7-14), the association with the older event allows both to take on a richer significance, with the new era fulfilling the promise of the old.

Ezra-Nehemiah

So far, then, the biblical texts reveal a range of possible ways of associating exodus and exile, by turns comforting, sobering, and frightening. Still another side also appears in the liturgical texts that connect exodus and exile. Some later texts show a discomfort with God's role in the association, even when they acknowledge Israel's culpability.

So Nehemiah 9 contains a long prayer that rehearses the foundational events of the exodus and migrations through the desert, coupling them with the much later deportations, which seem not so much to undo the exodus as to call into question its permanent relevance. Yet the prayer ends not with acceptance of exile or even a final explanation of it as a result of human evildoing. Rather, the prayer notes that while the community deported to Babylon has returned some of its members to the ancestral homeland, others remain far away. So in a rhetorically sophisticated move, the prayer appeals to God's sense of fair play:

> So now our God, the great, mighty and awesome God,
> you who keep covenant and loyalty,
> don't underestimate all the suffering that overtook us,
> our kings, nobles, priests, prophets, ancestors, and all your
> people.
> Since you are justified in all that's happened to us—
> for you did right, and we were wrong,
> and our kings, nobles, priests, and ancestors did not keep your
> Torah. . . .

However, we are slaves today;
and as for the land you gave our ancestors
so (we) could eat its pleasant fruit,
even here in it we are slaves. (Neh. 9:32–34a, 36)

The text fusses over a clear delineation of responsibility, politely refusing to blame God for continued separation from the homeland, the persistence of diaspora. It acknowledges the sins of the ancestors but insists on the proper weighing of responsibility. The ancestors sinned, yet the current generation of Israelites, who did not, still experience servitude in their own land.

That is, the prayer signals a strong cognitive dissonance, an awareness that the sort of reversal of exile and renewal of exodus that 1 Kings 8 and Isaiah 40–55 envision, albeit in different ways, did not literally come true, at least not for everyone. An unsettledness remains, not just in the physical separation of different parts of the Israelite community but in their state of mind or rather in the political and economic structures in which they lived, as well as in their theological confidence in Yahweh's willingness to deliver.

Exile did not end. Ever. Whether it would remained to be seen.

Some Implications:
Covenant Faithfulness and Mutual Obligations

It might seem strange, then, to point to these texts of exodus and exile in a larger discussion of the Bible's views of migration, whether forced, unforced, or something in-between. After all, the self-blame to which the texts call their Israelite listeners might seem to justify viewing such migrants as paying the price of their own decisions. Such a simplistic interpretation would force the modern reader either to accept the view of history as a penitentiary (in the etymological sense of that word as a place where one makes penance for wrongdoing) or to reject it altogether, abandoning the Bible as a resource for moral reflection on the topic of migration.

I say, "might seem to justify." In truth, the texts do not exhibit such a one-sided view of the matter. They all accept the idea that God acts in human history, interacting with human players as their passions for power exert themselves even against each other. Yet the God of Israel does not seem to be one player among many, not even the most powerful player. Rather, the deity operates by different rules altogether, rules that the prophets, historians, and singers of Israel sought to articulate. They did so in varied ways, creating a dialogue around a few key points. Just as the texts about *golah*, discussed earlier, speak of migration in international terms with various nations as victims and victimizers and something in-between, so also the texts connecting exodus and exile both hold humans accountable for events (thus freeing Israel from a sense of helplessness) and place responsibility for those same events just as squarely on Yahweh's shoulders. The texts appeal to the empathy of the deity and thereby foster empathy in their human readers as well.

What should we learn from this shifting discourse about the nature of movement and the mover? That the migrant may expect God's compassion as well as the imposition of moral demands? That the tendency of any religion to underwrite the status quo cannot survive the acids of either political movements or the relentless self-examination required of Israel's interactions with Yahweh? That the repetition of history in the movement to and from the promised land, and then back again, calls into question the permanence of any settlement and illustrates the precariousness of firm political boundaries and political arrangements? All of that comes from these texts and more.

Perhaps what cries out for attention most effusively in these texts and others like them is their focus on what the various actors owe each other. Whatever their stance toward the precise allotment of blame for the deportations on Israel, Yahweh, or the invading powers, all the biblical texts presuppose a notion of covenant faithfulness among the concerned parties. Israel lived in a relationship with Yahweh that entailed certain moral obligations. Yahweh could not break the deal even when Israel reneged on key parts of it.

Even the harshest indictments of Israel's sinfulness, the blaming of them for their own suffering, which seems so indefensible to modern readers, comes out of what David Novak nicely termed a "phenomenology of agreement," according to which God and humanity owe each other something.[6] We may disagree on the exact content of those mutual obligations, but the Israelite texts all presuppose the existence of a deeply enmeshed relationship among human beings and between them and God. We owe each other dignified treatment whether we recognize that obligation or not.

This relationship undergirds the ideas about human nature that operate throughout the Bible as well. These texts point to the untenability of dividing humanity into airtight categories of good and evil people, of sinners and saints. They also insist that national identity must move down the list of markers when considering the nature of human interactions. Israel's experience of deportation did not differ in kind from the experiences of other groups. The callused feet of marching hordes, the blood and sweat and aching muscles of dislocated people know neither religion nor language nor political commitments. Yet how we talk about those realities can vary, and talking about them in detail and accurately seems to matter.

Matter, how? The texts connecting exodus and exile as two instances of stories of Israel's migration show that narratives of migration are adaptable because they contain within themselves so many other stories; that these stories, in their complexity, create space for moral reflection; and that, nevertheless, storytelling alone may not trigger that reflection without the presence of another catalyst, whether earth-shaking historical events or an internal social process such as prophecy.

Perhaps most significantly, connecting two stories does not make them the same. Some biblical texts, such as Joshua–2 Kings, see the exodus and exile stories as bookends to a centuries-long historical process. Other texts see the deportations marking the end of the Israelite kingdoms more as interruptions of history, something difficult to explain, much less accept. But all these texts keep the stories separate, even while connecting them.

The texts that survive from Israel preserve the integrity of each story by what they include and omit. Omission first: it is surely interesting that the exodus story drew into its orbit many stories of events in the wilderness separating Egypt and Canaan. Some texts see the wilderness space as positive (e.g., Isa. 63:7-14; Jer. 2:2-3; Hos. 13:5-6; Amos 2:10), while the fullest treatment of the period, the book of Numbers, insists on its tragic dimensions by reporting the community's constant bickering as it wandered through a hostile environment.

On the other hand, the surviving texts speak hardly at all about the practical struggles of those who migrated, willingly or otherwise, in response to the Assyrian and Babylonian invasions. Their experiences would surely have supplied abundant material for storytelling and song, and yet such material does not exist.

To be sure, stories of later life in diaspora do come to us, including Esther's satire on life in the Persian royal court or the passion for family life in a hostile environment as seen in Tobit, as we will see.[7] Yet the biblical text falls surprisingly silent on their movements and their lives in the great expanses of land beyond the homeland. In part, this gap reflects an accident of literary production: the texts we have come from Jerusalem and perhaps other urban centers in the old northern and southern kingdoms. All writers adopt a perspective, and all write about what they know or can find out. So the geographic origin of the text may explain its geographic focus.

Yet this explanation does not cover all the bases, for several reasons. First, the groups that returned from their places of exile must inevitably have brought home stories of their time away. Moreover, as chapter seven will discuss, a two-way communication network existed, at least at times. A few prophetic texts mention that network and describe how key individuals took advantage of it to communicate their message. So authors in the land could have accessed stories from outside the homeland. The omission reflects a literary and perhaps theological choice rather than a gap in knowledge.

Moreover, as chapter five will argue, this absence may be less complete than it seems at first. Stories of the deportees' life may be hiding in unexpected places, including in the central Israelite story, the exodus itself. Stories of exodus and poems of exile connect, and from their connection emerges a basic perspective on what it means to be human.

CHAPTER 5

Exodus, Exile, and Human Nature

THE VISION OF HUMANITY as a species on the move, responsible for its own actions yet vulnerable to the decisions of others, influences stories about the exodus and poems about the exile. This association appears in two places in the Old Testament above all, in the book of Exodus and the part of the book of Isaiah often called the Second Isaiah, chapters 40–55. These texts presuppose the large and small in the lives of migrants and exiles: the quiet compromises with injustice, the day-to-day push to find edible food or a warm bed free of vermin, the hope for a kind word or a friendly face. The slaves contribute to the well-being of the larger culture, without reward or acknowledgment.

Behind the stories of the exodus lies a searching analysis of the workings of power, especially its tendency to grind human fodder for the insatiable hunger of the mighty seeking to make their own nation great again. But the analysis takes the form of story, not abstract philosophy. Israel did not search for first principles so much as find a way to bear witness to suffering created by the pretensions of leaders exploiting their people's fears. They told the stories of the slaves who built Pithom and Raamses, Egypt's storehouse cities, while leaving the pharaoh to whose glory they built them unnamed and unlamented.

Likewise, the poetry of deportation and return in the book of Isaiah speaks of God and kings while also capturing the anguish of powerless people who must dare to hope or, failing that, to face the abyss. The stories and poems together create the intellectual and spiritual environment from which the Bible's laws against oppressing the foreigner derive their meaning and purpose (see chap. 6).

The Book of Exodus

When Exodus 23:9 insists, then, that "you will not mistreat an alien [or migrant] because you know the alien's life since you were aliens in the land of Egypt," it appeals to a story. As always, law comes out of human experience and appeals to that experience, even when it is divine law. In the Old Testament legal traditions, neither individual laws nor the law as a magnificent whole descends straight from heaven, unfiltered by the realities of life on earth. Quite to the contrary.

In this case, "you know that you were aliens in the land of Egypt" appeals to Israel's collective memory and the cognitive processes for accessing that memory properly. In remembering, Israel must decide to equate their ancestors' sojourn in Egypt with the experiences of others now sojourning in Israel itself. They must also avoid the assumption that their past status as the suffering party exempted them from the potential of becoming the oppressor. Memory plus empathy equals justice. The sentence also calls out of that memory a story, the fullest presentation of which appears in the book in which the law also appears, Exodus.

This book of Exodus tells its story in several acts. In Act 1, an oppressed people find a deliverer, Yahweh, and a spokesperson for that deliverer, Moses (Exod. 1:1–15:21). In Act 2, these newly free people travel from their place of suffering through the desert to a rendezvous with their divine deliverer (Exod. 15:22–18:27). In Act 3, they hear God's word at Mount Sinai (Exod. 19:1–24:18), learning

64

for the first time the tunes and rhythms of freedom. In Act 4, they wrestle with the absence of the deliverer, who spends forty days talking with Moses about architecture, the construction of the tabernacle.

The discussion atop Sinai leads to the building of a mobile sanctuary (mobile because Israel remained mobile) where the divine-human encounter can take place on a sustained basis without the holy place becoming an end in itself. But this happy prospect does not happen without terrible conflict as the people seek to manage their movements by calling an idol "your gods, O Israel, who brought you from Egypt's land" (Exod. 32:4; cf. 1 Kings 12:28). The contrast between the ideal and the real reaches an unbearable tension that the text resolves by reintroducing Yahweh as the Holy One whose alternating presence and absence allow the people to find their bearings. And then the book ends with the overwhelming presence of the deity, whose glory filled the tabernacle (Exod. 40:34–38).

True, this synopsis of the plot of Exodus oversimplifies it considerably because the book's twists and turns explore the lives of certain key characters as they deal with the problems of migration and settlement. In particular, the words and actions of Yahweh, Moses, pharaoh, and the Israelites allow the book to probe the promises we make to each other and the ways in which covenants among accountable parties reveal their understanding of themselves and others (to refer again to Novak's ideas mentioned earlier). Pharaoh, Exodus insists, has broken Egypt's implied promises to the migrants it hosts, succumbing to greed and fear so that they have come to see national greatness as a zero-sum game won only at the expense of the vulnerable. How does this exploration of human relationships take place in narrative, then? How does the book of Exodus tell the story of migration from the points of view of the migrant, the host, and the deity who must superintend them all?

The Bad Host

Begin with the villain of the piece. Readers of Genesis remember that during a famine, the ancestors of Israel traveled from Canaan to the more prosperous superpower Egypt, counting on the bounty of the Nile to secure a reliable supply of grain. There, they found their relative Joseph in charge after a series of extraordinary coincidences. At the invitation of the crown, they settled down into a life at the edge of the kingdom, in Goshen, southeast of the delta, not as conquerors certainly and not really as assimilated Egyptians either. They remained "aliens" (Hebrew: *gerim*), both in the society and not quite part of it. There the text leaves them for an indeterminate period of time.

Then at last comes Exodus's fateful announcement, "a new king, who did not know Joseph, took over Egypt" (Exod. 1:8). The line does more than mark time, for of course the march of generations inevitably breaks the ties of memory. Old names become just that, labels for past relationships. The new king's lack of connection to Joseph involves more than the passage of time, however. He feels no obligation to carry out the promises of his predecessors when breaking them will accrue to him power and influence.

For an ancient society, such royal forgetfulness characterized a tyrant, not a foresighted leader. The promises of one generation obligated succeeding ones. A king ought not repeal the commitments of his predecessor to a family or a group of people simply out of spite or ambition or bloody-mindedness. (So the contemporary reneging on pledges of deferred action on childhood arrivals, the famous DACA, would have seemed grossly immoral and dishonorable to even the most ruthless ancient ruler and his people.) For example, David promised to defend Jonathan's descendants and did so even when he suspected one of them, Mephibosheth, of participating in insurrection (2 Sam. 19:24–30 [Hebrew 19:25–31]).

In fact, this expectation that a promise is a promise plays out in many ways in David's story, as when he has shown loyalty both to his natural overlord Saul and to Saul's mortal enemy Akish, the Philistine king of Gath. The storyteller must unravel that delicious conflict, brought about by Saul's growing madness and unreliability, by having the Philistine allies of Akish question David's loyalty and have him dismissed from the battlefield where the alliance would face a sore test (1 Sam. 29:1-7).

Further afield, prophets and historians speak of the ties of blood and commitment between Edom and Israel, or alliances between the Davidic dynasty and the Phoenicians of Tyre, or even international promises between Israelite rulers and their Assyrian masters. Violating any of those promises brought on divine wrath.[1] In at least some cases, ancient rulers saw themselves as members of a potential "relationship of friends— brothers—across hundreds of miles," as Amanda Podany has put it in her study of Near Eastern diplomacy just before the rise of Israel.[2] Loyalty equaled honor, a stance toward the world that, sadly, has eroded more recently.[3]

In other words, Exodus's simple statement of succession sets the stage for the following events, casting the new pharaoh's demagogic acts as a breach of a widely accepted way of ruling others. The text does not merely blame him for offending Israelites. It insists that his behavior violates more universal rules, and thus his cruelty deserves no excuse, no mitigation, no sympathy.

As the story proceeds, pharaoh commits his state to a policy of oppression, insisting that, "Truly Israel's children are a people mightier and more powerful than we. Let's be wise about them so they don't get bigger and whenever war breaks out they join our enemies and fight against us and then leave the land" (Exod. 1:9-10). This demagogic harangue exposes a longstanding approach to the foe within. Here the ruler brands a group in his territory as a potential enemy, not because of anything they have done but because of their alienness. For pharaoh, only two classes of people exist: them and us. Everyone in the box marked "them" works together against "us." Today's immigrant becomes tomorrow's enemy. Alienness cannot be bridged by personal commitments, years or even generations of life together, legal and moral commitments to one another's well-being. So works the unscrupulous ruler, the moral bankrupt at the top of the society, the leader who cannot imagine that the immigrant needs protection from the host country rather than the reverse. Sanctuary cities anyone?

A contradiction in the rhetoric leads to the specific policies of oppression: "they might leave." Surely the narrative foreshadows the events that follow,[4] the exodus itself, and yet something else rings true. The demonization of the alien group, the lie about their superior power and willingness to ally with others against their hosts, goes hand in hand with a fear that they might leave. The contradiction can only be resolved by enslaving them, ensuring that their danger can be tamed or rather channeled in an economically useful direction.

And so pharaoh reduces previously free people to servitude. There they remain until a new character enters the drama.

Many years ago, Edmund Wilson described Karl Marx's tendency to control others by noting that "it is exceedingly difficult for one whose deepest internal existence is all a wounding and being wounded, a crushing and being crushed, to conceive, however much he may long for, a world ruled by peace and fraternity, external relations between men based on friendliness, confidence and reason."[5] Whether that verdict convicts Marx or not, it applies far more amply to Exodus's pharaoh. Such a man cannot back away from the patterns of government that translate human hatred into policy and action. In cultures with cults of the leader as strong as ancient Egypt's always was and as its neighbors perceived it to be, the wounding and being wounded could hardly avoid extending to the entire political system.

Based on a searching analysis of such a reality, and to highlight the absence of "peace and fraternity," the Exodus storytellers focus in on a single family of the now-enslaved migrants. This sort of move is typical of biblical narrative, with most stories concentrating on two or three characters and bringing them in or out of the story in order to let it move forward with the fewest possible obstructions. Brilliant, spare storytelling as a literary technique underscores in this case the austere hardship faced by the people themselves.

Here we see a mother of young children forced to save her infant boy from a royal decree to drown the male Israelite children (much as one culls a herd of cattle of its excess male members for breeding purposes). Her forlorn hope puts the child in a basket and places him on the banks of the Nile. And by the way, the state-sponsored murder of baby boys also puts at risk their sisters and mothers, now more likely to become the sex objects of the dominant culture, much as Sarah found herself. The Egyptian state's policy of atrocity put everyone at risk, since no one may claim the legitimate protection of the state from arbitrary violence. Rather, says the book of Exodus, Egypt has rejected the ancient Near Eastern idea that the ruler must protect the vulnerable from the strong.

Since the reader knows the happy ending of this scene, with the baby finding a home with a princess conveniently bathing in the Nile, it is easy to overlook the horror of the moment. The text, of course, does not let us see inside the mother's mind or hear her anguished cries for help, her arguments with herself, her nagging fears until the moment of rescue. She must count on the compassion of her oppressors, hoping that a conscience exists in at least one of them.

But the storyteller forces us to notice these very human possibilities by not pointing them out explicitly. We must decide whether our empathy for Jochebed and her son Moses suffices to place us next to her, or perhaps to turn a blind eye to her pain in order to accept the majestic logic of a ruler convinced that might and right both lie on his side if only he can remove the living, breathing reminder that it does not.

Thanks to the generosity of an anonymous princess who goes down in history as a righteous Gentile, the baby grows into a man, Moses, who looms over Exodus and the rest of the Bible as a titanic figure. Miracle-worker, lawgiver, warrior, a man who can persuade God—all these elements mark Moses out as heroic. Yet he also appears in the stories about him as perhaps the first recognizably human figure in all literature. A man of complex emotions, and not a hero "two-thirds a god" like the older Gilgamesh, whose physical prowess could overcome the weakness of mind, Moses appears in all these stories consciously wrestling with his own fears and hopes.

Some of those fears include the nature of his people as a migrant people. In the decisive story of his call to prophethood in Exodus 3-4, he hears Yahweh's pitch for liberation with its careful diagnosis of the problems facing Israel as a hosted migrant community, as well a proposal for its solution. Yahweh's self-introduction highlights the link to the migrating families:

> I am the God of your ancestor:
> the God of Abraham,
> the God of Isaac,
> and the God of Jacob. (Exod. 3:6)

Then follows the diagnosis of Israel's dilemma, an act of bearing witness to the sufferings of an alien population in a land whose fear and power-mongering have led it to make victims of its erstwhile guests: "I have certainly seen the affliction of my people that is in Egypt. I have heard their cry on account of their slave drivers. Indeed, I know their pains. So I will descend to save them from Egyptian control in order to bring them up from that land to a good and broad land, to the land flowing with milk and honey" (Exod. 3:7-8).

See. Hear. Know. Yahweh appeals to sources of knowledge comparable to human sense perceptions in order to bear witness first to Moses, then to the hearers of the tale about the plight of the migrants. The solution to their plight will eventually be more movement.

Yet things are not so simple. Moses, of course, sympathizes with the plight of his kinspeople and cheers on their rescue until he realizes his own responsibility toward them. He cannot deliver them. He can only speak on their behalf. But this he must do in spite of his objections ("Who am I?" "Who are you?" "They won't believe me!"), all of which reflect both the particulars of the exodus moment and the terrifying magnitude of the demands the task places upon him. To rescue even one soul from death marks a person's life as worthwhile. To rescue thousands—that's another matter.

This call of Moses introduces another important theme in Israel's self-understanding as a migrant people, their own group psychology, as it were. Both Yahweh and Moses bear witness to the people's suffering as the victims of a legal and economic system in which their existence provided an excuse for terror. Yet Moses knows the limitations of these people. He does not see them as noble simply because of their suffering. Oppression robs both ruler and ruled of dignity. Nobility must follow redemption. This is why Moses asks for God's real name, so that he can convince the people of the legitimacy of his prophetic mission and give them the courage to embrace their own liberation.

Moses put the uncertainty that he and Israel feel about Yahweh's promises most clearly a little later in the story, after he has failed to persuade pharaoh at their initial encounter and even provoked the tyrant to increase the workload of the oppressed migrants. Pan the cameras to the next encounter between Moses and Yahweh:

> And Moses spoke this way to Israel's children, but they would not listen to Moses because of their depressed soul and their brutal servitude. Then Yahweh responded to Moses, "Go speak to pharaoh, Egypt's king, so he can send Israel's children from his land." Moses replied to Yahweh, "Look, Israel's children haven't listened to me, so how will pharaoh listen to me when I have uncircumcised lips?"[6] (Exod. 6:9-12)

The narrator insists that the oppressed people lack courage but attributes that lack not to any sort of internal character flaw but to the external conditions of their lives, conditions created by the decisions of state power. The pitiless rules of the Egyptian government have ground down the people of Israel so that they cannot believe even in their own salvation. Yahweh must carry the messenger, and through him the people, to an alternative view.

Of course, Yahweh does manage to bring them forward, but not before terrible conflicts. The steady drumbeat of the ten plagues rings across the text as blood, frogs, gnats, flies, and the rest systematically dismantle the system of wealth creation dependent on slave labor as well as the bounty of nature. The repeated disasters reveal the character of the two kings in the drama: the human king, pharaoh, proves to be an unreliable partner in any deal making since he repeatedly weasels out of promises to let the people go. Yahweh, on the other hand, proves implacably committed to the task of rescuing the migrants.

Finally, Israel leaves Egypt, though not alone. Accompanying them, a "great multitude" of non-Israelites bring along their own possessions (Exod. 12:38).[7] While the succeeding narratives reveal little of their stories, the fact that the text speaks simply of "the congregation of Israel" or some such group would indicate a merger of the whole. DNA proved less crucial than moral and religious behavior.

Rather than making its victims into virtuous heroes and its villains into inhuman monsters, Exodus prefers to report what Hannah Arendt famously called the banality of evil. Pharaoh seems to have no master plan for his master race. He simply lies and evades until he no longer can. Israel brings to the fore no brave heroes, only ordinary people whose souls are crushed but who somehow manage to persevere. Even Yahweh, neither banal nor evil, still appears as simultaneously brutal in crushing the host country Egypt and compassionate toward the migrant people Israel. That brutality appears inescapable given the utter cruelty of the Egyptian system.

Exodus picks up the already ancient theme of conflict between a deity and what we would call forces of nature (though ancient people saw them as living beings like the gods). It transforms that theme not only by having Yahweh part the sea (Exod. 14–15) but by crushing a human foe who pretends that his power entitles him to mistreat other human beings.[8]

Hence the book of Exodus. The book sets up the legal discussions of the Pentateuch by telling a story. This fact should not surprise anybody. Human beings understand the world through our stories about ourselves operating in it. How we tell the story comes out of our deepest values and also either corrects or reinforces those very values. Law comes from a broader underlying morality, morality derives from most basic human interconnectedness, and that interconnectedness flows from the creative work of God. (Chapter six will take up that point.) Religion can underwrite revolution by bearing witness to the suffering of people and holding out hope for their deliverance. And that is what Exodus does.

From Exodus to Exile and Back Again

The book of Exodus, then, offers an anatomy of tyranny. Oppressive states mark out "the other" as a source of danger that needs control, usually by a combination of economic exploitation, sexual and physical abuse, and finally violence or even murder. But the book does something more. It stakes out a path for hope, to which it calls its readers. With a clear-eyed realism, the stories of Exodus recognize that enslavement can rob people of the capacity for self-preservation, even with a supernatural boost. Yet hope may survive and grow so as to rekindle the human flame.

Building hope is also the task that the poet who composed Isaiah 40–55 took up, in part by reclaiming the language of the exodus for a new era. But before we get to that text, a brief detour on the word *hope* might help.

In a recent philosophical exploration of hope, Adrienne Martin argues that it is not a sort of irrational feeling but a reasonable stance to which we come when we believe that a desired outcome is possible but not certain (the chances are between 0 and 100 percent). That is, no sane person "hopes" to acquire the ability to fly under her own power or, conversely, "hopes" that the sun will rise tomorrow morning. The first is impossible, the second inevitable.

More than that, Martin argues, the existence of hope in a person leads him or her to mount a defense of that hope and to act upon it. So if I hope that the treatment for cancer I'm beginning can cure me, even if the chances remain low, I will act in ways that reflect that hope and justify my actions to others. Hope transforms both my inner state and my external actions and relationships with others. As Martin puts it,

> The hopeful person takes a "licensing" stance toward the probability she assigns the hoped-for outcome—she sees that proba-

bility as licensing her to treat her desire for the outcome and the outcome's desirable features as reasons to engage in the forms of planning, thought, and feeling [already discussed]. . . . The second part of hope's incorporation element is the hopeful person actually treating her desire and the outcome's desirable features as reasons to engage in said forms of planning, thought, and feeling.[9]

For Martin, hope need not be religious (though it can be), but it does profoundly shape how an individual interacts with the world. Hope differs from wishful thinking in that it leads to a way of conducting life that connects the subjective experience of desiring to the objective nature of the thing desired in a way that can be acted upon. Again, reasonable people can hope.

This helpful discussion of Martin's does not, however, distinguish among the sorts of things for which one might hope. Certainly to escape the ravages of cancer or to live long enough to see one's grandchildren would not strike anyone as unreasonable. Having enough food to eat, finding safety for one's family or friends, avoiding violence from others, gaining access to education—all of these hopes seem so uncontroversial that we frequently speak of them as rights. On the other hand, some hopes seem so problematic that we rightly make laws against them, even when whole societies have at times embraced them. The quest for racial "purity" or the desire to colonize weaker cultures comes to mind, for example.

What we hope for, how we justify that hope, and how we act upon that justification all matter. So does finding language to express that hope. These intersubjective expressions of hope matter, indeed, for the text that takes up the exodus idea most amply and transfers it to a new historical situation, the return of some of Israel's deported population to its ancestral homeland. That text is Isaiah 40-55.

This cycle of poems draws heavily on the earlier poetry of Isaiah (chaps. 1-39) as it builds out a vision of a postdeportation world. During the late sixth century, about which and probably during which the poetry of Isaiah 40-55 was written, the Babylonian Empire slid into the much larger Persian Empire, which the brilliant king Cyrus had built from scratch. One of the great conquerors of history, Cyrus cobbled together a realm stretching from the Indus Valley to Macedonia. The Levantine coast and the nearby hill country regions of Jerusalem and Samaria, the onetime kingdoms of Judah and Israel, were among his possessions, probably minor in his calculations even if significant for their position at the border with the still independent kingdom of Egypt and athwart important trade routes.[10]

These lands seemed small to him perhaps, but enormous to those who, like the Second Isaiah, called them home, even from afar. Cyrus comes down in Jewish history as the great liberator, the ruler who undid almost two centuries of Assyrian and Babylonian policy of deportation. He sent the deportees home to rebuild their ancestral cities, replant the old farmlands, and worship the old gods. The policy of repatriation embraced many peoples, including the Israelites.

In order to find language to speak about the revolution in Israel's fate, the mash-up of poems in Isaiah 40-55 uses old language and ideas in new ways. The opening lines construct a conversation among various voices that speak of how "our God's word stands up forever" (Isa. 40:8), continuing to insist that the other gods did not predict Israel's reversal of fortune and the accompanying defeat of the Babylonian superstate (e.g., Isa. 41:21-24; 44:6-8, 24-25; 45:20-23; 46:1-13). Therefore, that empire's religious rationales for their conquests fail to persuade in the long run. Idols can neither save nor guide history.

The imperial view had always assumed that migrants deserved their fate and that their existence served the needs of the state and the dominant culture behind it. This view, says the Second Isaiah, has collapsed of its own contradictions. So the poetry affirms, and the historical movements of the time confirm.

Along with a detailed discussion of Yahweh's superiority and graciousness toward the deportees, and an explanation of the change of geopolitical power as the work of deity, the poetry draws on the language of the exodus. So the joyous lines paint a picture of a situation when

The needy and the poor seek water, but there is none.
Their tongue is parched with thirst.
Then I, Yahweh, answer them—
as Israel's God I do not abandon them.
I open up riverbanks, springs out of the hills.
I turn the desert to swamp, dry land to streams of water.

(Isa. 41:17-18)

The theme of ecological upgrade stands in for human renewal all over the book of Isaiah, as it does here.[11] That language links the return from Babylonia to the exodus and wilderness traditions, and becomes clearer in a text like Isaiah 48:20-21 as it reminds the poet's audience of Yahweh's proclivity toward dramatic miracles:

Leave Babylon, flee the Chaldeans.
With loud singing, announce, proclaim this,
bring the news to the earth's end.
Say, "Yahweh has redeemed his servant Jacob.
They did not thirst when he brought them through wastelands.
He made water gush from the rock for them,
and split the rock so water flowed."

The lines evoke the wanderings through the desert after the exodus, emphasizing not so much Israel's cantankerous behavior, a major theme in the book of Numbers, but the mercy of God who cares for basic human needs. The poet thus concludes the first major section of the poems (Isa. 40-48) by bearing witness to past saving deeds of God and connecting them to the present return from Babylon. The reader must also join in the testimony, offering both a reason for hope (God has acted this way before) and a plan of action (movement back to the homeland).

The connection becomes clearer still in the elaborate discussion of chapter 49, the opening of the second major section of the poems. After acknowledging that a dispirited audience may fail to hear the hopeful message (much as their ancestors refused to hear the original Isaiah's call to repentance), the poet insists that redeemed Israel will exist not simply for its own sake, surely a good thing in itself, but as a "light to the nations so that my salvation may reach the end of the earth" (Isa. 49:6).

The text goes on to promise smooth roads for the migrants to travel home, their trip watered by "springs of water" (Isa. 49:10) as in stories of the trip through the wilderness in the exodus story. It then describes an extraordinary reversal of fortune.

In an oracle announcing salvation, the poet quotes Yahweh as saying,

> Yes, I will raise my hand to the nations, lift my banner to peoples, and bring back my sons in the bosom, my daughters lifted on shoulders.
> Yes, kings will be your guardians and princesses your wet nurses. They will prostrate themselves to you, and lick the dust of your feet.
> And then you will know that I am Yahweh. (Isa. 49:22–23)

"Then you will know that I am Yahweh" echoes the theme of discovering God's identity seen also in Exodus. But here the poet goes much further than the older texts. In the vision that emerges, foreign rulers will no longer threaten, no longer manage oppressive political systems, no longer amass power for its own sake, no longer use the refugees and deportees as pawns in their political maneuvers. Rather, they will both obey ("lick the dust") and provide much-needed nurture ("wet nurses"), thus taking up the roles the Israelites themselves had assumed.

But not yet. All this renewal of the promise lies in the near future. For now, the poet must turn again to prayer for Yahweh's help, resorting to the language of the exodus. So Isaiah 51:9–11 presents a prayer reminiscent of various war songs (Judg. 5:12; Pss. 7:7 [English 7:6]; 44:24 [English 44:23]; 59:5 [English 59:4]), with either a human being or God as a warrior needing to wake up for battle. As the call to Yahweh the divine warrior puts it,

Awake, awake, gird on strength, O Yahweh's arm!
Awake as in olden days, times long ago.
Aren't you the one that struck Rahab, the twisty sea monster?
Aren't you the one that evaporated the sea, the mighty waters
    of the deep,
the one who turned the sea into a path for the redeemed to cross
    over?
So shall Yahweh's ransomed ones turn around and go to Zion
    with shouting,
    with constant joy on their head.
Singing and joy will overtake them. Sorrow and moaning will
    disappear.

For this poet, the return from the land of deportation in some ways surpasses the exodus.

This last small poem draws on the old pre-Israelite imagery of the creator god's battle with chaotic forces. Victory makes creation possible. As in several other texts, that original story of creation underscores Yahweh's might and grace (Job 9:13; 26:12; Ps. 89:11 [English 89:10]), and here it merges with the exodus story of the crossing of the sea ("a path for the redeemed to cross over"). Creation, exodus, exile, and return all become different episodes in a single story of divine wonder aimed at the benefit of a migratory people.

The Dignity and Moral Responsibility of the Migrant

Of course, much more remains to be said about the presentation of the exodus story in the book of Exodus and its reclamation for a new era in Isaiah 40–55. But already several points have emerged that both reveal Israel's thinking and point contemporary readers of the Bible toward constructive viewpoints.

First, both Exodus and Isaiah 40–55 analyze political structures and leaders in realistic ways without believing in their ultimate legitimacy. These texts, and the Israelite tradition more generally, deeply distrust the exertions that states make for power and the ways in which they legitimate those exertions. States always need an "other" against which they can make their claims. To put matters crudely, we could say "no threat, no army, no structures supporting that army, no grandeur for leaders." Migrant groups provide convenient "others" to intimidate, control, and use for various economic, military, and political purposes. Yet one should always suspect the rhetoric about these others as illusions that states and their leaders create for ulterior purposes.

Yet, second, these texts insist that such political rhetoric ultimately fails, collapsing because of its own internal contradictions, and in some instances at least because God intervenes on behalf of the dislocated persons. The revolution that the various Israelite texts espouse comes from high above humanity, not from below. At the same time, these texts do not see religion as escape from the challenges of life, but as a tool for mastering them.

Third, in the revolution of the spirit that both Exodus and Isaiah 40–55 envision, the value of the displaced, the migrants without a country, cannot be determined by their economic value. Indeed, the state may not decide their value at all. That assessment comes from God alone. These texts, therefore, take a radical stance as they insist that the migrant's self-definition must befit his or her dignity as a human being before God.

Fourth, both of these texts wrestle with assigning guilt and innocence. Like other prophetic texts, they realize that labels for moral accountability run in a continuum. "Sinner" and "saint" do not constitute airtight categories. But at the same time, blame and praise do not ultimately apply. For example, Isaiah 40–55 accepts the earlier claims of Isaiah 1–39 that the deported Israelites bear some responsibility for their own fate. Yet that responsibility does not stop Yahweh from bearing witness to their suffering and making moves to stop and then reverse it. How much more so does Exodus, which blames the enslavement in Egypt solely on the Egyptians and contextualizes Israel's later inability to obey Torah as a result of the experience of oppression. In other words, both texts engage in a complex internal discussion about the nature of the moral agency of even oppressed people. This moral responsibility-

economic value does not determine dignity/value

taking, as I argued in chapter three, actually liberates the displaced people from a sense of helplessness and the dehumanization of low expectations.

Fifth, and finally, both Exodus and Isaiah 40-55 take seriously their own nature as texts that must appeal to energized audiences. They invite readers into a culture of empathy by which those who live at home feel a deep solidarity with those who do not. While both texts focus upon Israelite migrants—they are after all Israelite texts—they do not espouse a narrow nationalism. Exodus can acknowledge unhesitatingly the presence of non-Israelites among the crowd following Moses, and Isaiah 56, in a sort of coda to Isaiah 40-55, explicitly welcomes foreigners and eunuchs to the reconstituted Jerusalem community as long as they observe the Sabbath and honor Yahweh. So, while these texts concern Jewish history first of all, they do not exhaust their hopes for the end of suffering through migration on Israelites alone. Rather, together they spell out the preconditions for the legal system that arose in Israel according to which the migrant earns protection and a viable place in the larger society. That story in itself deserves attention.

Solidarity = we are all apart of the same family

Solidarity = we have a common goal

How do we achieve common goals with people different from us?

CHAPTER 6

The Law of the Stranger

So far we have heard the stories of migrants to and from Israel's homeland, whether the ancient ancestors or the exodus people or their distant descendants suffering through shifting imperial policies in the mid-first millennium BCE. These stories explore life as migrant and, to a lesser degree, host of migrants. That latter role takes center stage in another genre of Israelite literature, law.

For many people, the word *law* conjures up a confusion of associations, from TV courtroom dramas to our latest speeding ticket. Christians in particular enjoy a love-hate relationship with "law," which Martin Luther (unfortunately) taught us to contrast unfavorably with "gospel." Yet as most other Christian thinkers have realized, law's foes are tyranny and anarchy, not salvation.

How to appreciate biblical law, then? Understanding law requires attention to its contexts, both the history behind the words and the relationship of a given law to the other laws on related subjects. Simply parading proof texts to support one's case will not succeed when the judge possesses intelligence and integrity. Interpretation is required because law exists in a social environment of its own, complete with rules for how to implement the rules, personnel to make it work, and long-standing customs that connect the words on the page to practices and values of real life. Law reflects the values of a culture, as well as challenging them. Mere regulations achieve little in the absence of just judges and administrators, but a rule of law makes a good life possible. Interpretation must take account of all these factors.

To illustrate the point, Joseph Story, the great nineteenth-century legal scholar and Associate Justice of the United States Supreme Court from 1811 to 1845, once described the task of interpreting law this way:

> Where the words are plain and clear, and the sense distinct and perfect arising on them, there is generally no necessity to have recourse to other means of interpretation. It is only, when there is some ambiguity or doubt arising from other sources, that interpretation has its proper office. There may be obscurity, as to the meaning, from the doubtful character of the words used, from other clauses in the same instrument, or from an incongruity or repugnancy between the words, and the apparent intention derived from the whole structure of the instrument, or its avowed object. In all such cases interpretation becomes indispensable.[1]

For Story, the interpreter of law must pay attention to the overall structure of the text, not just its surface. Obscurity may come from unclear drafting of the text because of the complexity of the subject, the need to compromise among various stakeholders, or simply a lawyer's incompetence. Law reflects the values of a given society as well as its challenges. The removal of "ambiguity or doubt" must drive the interpretation of the law.

For ancient Israelite law, the need for interpretation comes from the same sort of sources. Legal texts bounce off each other, sometimes quoting, sometimes modifying, sometimes ignoring prior statements of norms. Indeed, the Bible does not contain a single legal code, but seven distinguishable collections that overlapped to some extent while also showing independent thought arising from the evolving needs of the society. These collections include

- The Ten Commandments (Exod. 20:1-17; Deut. 5:1-22 [English 5:1-21])
- The Covenant Code (Exod. 21:1-23:33)
- The Ritual Decalogue (Exod. 34:10-26)
- The Priestly Code (Lev. 1:1-16:34 plus several laws in Numbers)
- The Holiness Code (Lev. 17:1-27:34)
- The Deuteronomic Code (Deut. 12:1-26:19)
- The Curses Code (Deut. 27:11-26)

The laws in Deuteronomy extensively reinterpret the older Covenant Code, not willy-nilly, but according to clearly determined principles.[2] The Priestly and Holiness collections continue the process of interpretation even further.

All of these except the so-called Ritual Decalogue, a graciously reorienting response to the Golden Calf episode, include one or more statements about the responsibility of the Israelite community toward the *ger* ("migrant" or "alien," related to the verb *gur*, "to sojourn as a migrant"). Often the laws link these outsiders to the widow and orphan as categories of people who both need and deserve the protection of the judicial system and the society at large. Israel's legal texts exhibit a long-term, multifaceted concern for non-Israelites within the larger community. While these laws differ in some details, they all reflect a single-minded commitment to ensure the well-being of the migrants living alongside the host community and sharing in its most crucial commitments.

The Stranger (*ger*) in the Covenant Code

The oldest law collection seems to be the Covenant Code, which other biblical law collections comment on, amplify, and at times modify. These laws work for harmony in an agrarian society of small villages lacking a central authority. As in other law collec-

ger = migrant

tions in the Bible, this "code" makes no effort at being systematic. The text ignores many possible topics, and the processes for deciding cases and punishment of criminals go unexplained, probably because the methods of judging cases at the village level had gone on adequately for generations.[3]

In spite of the spotty coverage of topics, this collection of laws twice refers to the *ger*. In the first instance, the prohibition of idolatry leads to instructions about vulnerable people. In no uncertain terms, the law insists that "You should not oppress the *ger* nor abuse that person, for you were *gerim* in Egypt's land. Nor should you oppress a widow or an orphan. If you oppress such a person, when they cry out to me [in prayer], I will certainly answer them, and I will be infuriated and kill you at sword point. Then your wives will be widows and your children orphans" (Exod. 22:20–23 [English 22:21-24]).

As in other texts, the law links three different classes of people into what we might call the triad of the vulnerable. The *ger*, like the widow and the orphan, lacks the kind of family support that can protect an individual from mistreatment. The migrant flies about without a safety net. Without social support, these persons must rely even more heavily than usual on the social structures outside, or larger than, the family.

This law differs from the norm in an important way. Ordinarily biblical law either prescribes a penalty that the judicial system must carry out, or it spells out no punishment at all, relying on longstanding custom to carry the day. This law, however, takes neither approach but insists simply that abuse of the vulnerable will meet punishment from an angry God, who will personally assume the role of family avenger of wrong. "I will be infuriated and kill you at sword point," though marvelously unambiguous, stands out as an unusual statement in Israelite law or its Near Eastern parallels (such as the Code of Hammurabi). Usually, ancient texts think of God supporting law in general rather than individual rules. But here God intervenes directly to implement a law. For this text, then, mistreatment of the migrant, the widow, and the orphan differs in kind from other crimes precisely because these people lack reliable social defenses.

The Covenant Code also contains another law about the *ger*. Following a series of prohibitions of bribery and influence peddling, Exodus 23:9 insists "you shall not oppress a *ger* because you know the *ger*'s life since you were *gerim* in Egypt's land." It then transitions into rules about proper uses of time (for fallowing land and observing religious holidays). It does not specify the meaning of *oppress*, though in the context it must have something to do, at a minimum, with abuses of the court system that deprive the migrant of rights in favor of other parties to lawsuits. In other words, the migrant has rights in law more or less identical to those of Israelites. Neither judges nor the populace at large may circumvent those rights.

The curious thing about this law, however, is the warrant. Israelites should avoid abusing the *ger* not primarily out of fear of divine punishment (as in the law a few lines earlier), but because of empathy for the migrant's vulnerability. Whereas the law in Exodus 22 draws upon the experience of warfare as an expression of divine wrath ("at sword point," "widows," "orphans"), the law in Exodus 23 appeals to the better angels of Israel's nature. True, the latter law implies a threat: countries that oppress migrants can pay a heavy price when Yahweh gets involved. Yet compassion for the suffering of others motivates better than simple terror. Also, a reminder of the past forces the audience to consider a possible future for themselves: we could become like the Egyptians if we act as they did. We would then be not the beneficiaries of the exodus, but the villains against which the drama must replay itself.

An additional point here: the laws of the Covenant Code do not clarify the origins of the *ger*. In some cases, since ancient societies did not conceive of citizenship as we do and often thought more of one's home village or tribe than participation in an entire nation, the law may cover both migrants from outside Israel and those who reside far from home but nevertheless are Israelite. The laws do not make such a fine, Westphalian sort of distinction, though undoubtedly most *gerim* were non-Israelites.[4]

Nor do they distinguish among poor and nonpoor migrants, much less legal and illegal migrants, since those categories did not exist in ancient Israel. In an agrarian society of small landhold-ings that stayed in families over many generations, the potential for growing wealth remained limited for most people, migrant or not. Many migrants would have remained poor. Some scholars have attempted to describe the *gerim* as a social underclass, more or less like the noncitizen metics of ancient Athens or even a sort of lumpenproletariat, the poorest of the poor.[5] However, just as wid-ows could sometimes prosper, and orphans could inherit a fortune, at least a few migrants may have enjoyed some measure of financial success as merchants or soldiers. That is, a purely economic model may not map neatly onto the law. Yet by and large, the three groups of vulnerable people—widow, orphan, and *ger*—lacked the natural protection of family connections and thus faced potential discrimi-nation and abuse. They could easily lose their property to fraudsters and bullies. Hence the laws against such behaviors.

The Stranger (*ger*) in Deuteronomy

The later law collections of the Pentateuch draw on the Covenant Code for some of their basic orientations, often expanding or mod-ifying the older laws to fit new circumstances or previously uncon-sidered problems. The laws for migrants were no exception.

Most notably, the book of Deuteronomy refers to the *ger* no fewer than twenty-one times, in each with an aim of protecting their rights. The book consists of a legal collection (chaps. 12–26) inside an envelope of moral exhortation (chaps. 1–11; 29–33), with a smaller law code in chapter 27, blessings and curses in chapter 28, and the final scene of the Pentateuch, the death of Moses in chapter 34. That is, the book combines several types of material in a complex whole. So it is helpful to look at the work's component parts to understand its overall viewpoint.

The legal code proper refers to the *ger* fourteen times, in a va-riety of contexts. Consider these examples.

First, the food laws prohibit Israelites from consuming an an-imal that has died on its own (in part to maintain ritual purity) but allows a *ger* to do so (Deut. 14:21). That law also introduces a third category, the *nokri*, a foreigner who has not settled among Israelites but either passes through or maintains a separate existence disconnected socially from them. To that person, one may *sell* a corpse, whereas the *ger* may receive it gratis. The gift may seem dubious to modern Americans with our regular meat supply, but to ancient people, matters would undoubtedly have appeared differently.

Second, the law of the tithe insists that several people who do not own their own land must share in the communal meal. These include the Levite (for Deuteronomy, those who cannot officiate at the temple in Jerusalem but live in the villages), the widow, the orphan, and the *ger* (Deut. 14:29). Again, these migrants live alongside other members of the Israelite community.

Third, the laws regarding festivals make provision for non-Israelites. The rules for Shavuot or Pentecost invite the *gerim* to participate fully in the larger community's ritual celebrating the crops growing in their fields. So Deuteronomy 16:11 sets the tone for the festival by insisting that "You shall rejoice before Yahweh your God—you, and your son, your daughter, your male servant, your female servant, the Levite in your gates, the *ger*, the orphan, the widow among you—in the place where Yahweh your God will choose to make his name dwell." Likewise, Deuteronomy 16:14 extends that same list of celebrants to the festival of Sukkot or Tabernacles, which occurs in the fall and commemorates the migration through the wilderness after the exodus. When these people can celebrate in Jerusalem itself ("the place where Yahweh your God will choose to make his name dwell"),[6] they can join the larger community in celebrating ("rejoice") God's goodness to them. Israel does not merely tolerate the presence of these people without an immediate family connection, but invites them into a joyful life together.

Fourth, Deuteronomy 23:3-8 states rules limiting the participation of some foreigners in certain religious activities. Moabites and Ammonites, some of Israel's nearest neighbors, ought not enter the community's assembly for worship "unto the tenth generation"

87

because of their ancestors' brutal treatment of the Israelites as they migrated from Egypt to Canaan. On the other hand, the law demands that "you shall not abominate an Egyptian because you were a *ger* in their land" and concludes that "sons born to them up to the third generation will enter Yahweh's assembly."

One could be excused for finding this law confusing. It presupposes intermarriage (or at least sex and childbearing) between Israelites and foreigners, since it counts children with a foreign ancestor back to a certain generation as still foreign. It seems clear, moreover, that the law did not quite reflect practice, since King David himself, surely no mean Israelite, had a Moabite great-grandmother (Ruth 4:21-22). Perhaps one could reconcile these two facts by noting that Israelites early on traced descent in the male line, in contrast to the practice that began in the Second Temple period of tracing it through the female line. In that case, the "tenth generation" would count descent from an Ammonite or Moabite male, rather than a female. Perhaps.

But the more interesting point may be the contrast between the Ammonites and Moabites, on the one hand, and the Egyptians, on the other. All of these groups had abused Israel's ancestors. In the latter case, Egyptian heritage disqualified one only for three generations "because you were a *ger* in their land." In other words, the victimization in the wilderness surpassed in horror the experience of slavery in Egypt. The brutality of bondage came from a society accustomed to such behavior, locked into its own fear and passion for power. The brutality in the wilderness from Ammon and Moab lacked even that justification.

However one reads this law—and unanimity has by no means emerged over the centuries—the law does not prohibit intermarriage even with the three named groups. It does not limit children from other relationships with foreigners in any way. And so even at its most restrictive, Israelite law shows keen awareness of the risks of xenophobia and seeks to limit its effects.

Fifth, a cluster of laws protecting migrants and other workers appears in Deuteronomy 24:14-22. In a progressive bit of legislation, the text enjoins employers:

You shall not mistreat the poor or needy employee, whether one of your brothers [i.e., a fellow Israelite] or your migrant in your land, in your gates [i.e., city limits]. Pay them their wages each day. Don't let the sun set, because that person is poor and life itself may depend on it. Don't let him call out to Yahweh against you, for that would be a sin for you.

The parents should not die for something the children have done, nor children die for something the parents have done. Each person should die for his or her own sin.

Do not stretch out[7] the case of the *ger* or orphan, and do not take the widow's clothing as collateral. Rather, you should remember that you were a servant in Egypt, yet Yahweh your God redeemed you from there. Therefore, I am commanding you to do this thing.

When you harvest your field, and you miss a bundle of grain in the field, don't return to collect it. Leave it for the *ger*, orphan, or widow so that Yahweh your God will bless you in all your activities.

When you pick your olive groves, don't pick them clean. Leave some for the *ger*, the orphan, and the widow. Remember that you were a servant in Egypt's land. Therefore I am commanding you to do this thing.

These laws presuppose that private ownership of property does not entitle the owner to ignore social obligations. Hoarding, blocking access to one's land, and ignoring the plight of others are forbidden because Israel's core identity as a people liberated them from just such sharp divisions between the haves and the have-nots. Practical concerns for the survival of vulnerable people take precedence over any excess profits that more thorough exploitation of resources might make possible.

These laws assume that the *gerim*, like widows and orphans, lack strong family connections and thus a secure place in the economic system. They are poor day laborers and so need legal protection. Exploiting them betrays Israel's story as a liberated people and invites divine anger. The warning "Don't let them call out to

Yahweh against you" reminds the reader that prayer for help from oppression, so common in the book of Psalms and other parts of the Bible, draws Yahweh's attention because Yahweh has committed to maintaining justice among human beings, irrespective of their origins or social relationships.

Sixth, Deuteronomy's law code concludes with instructions about offerings and tithes, which the people should share with each other and God freely and joyfully. The gaggle of participants that appeared at festivals in Deuteronomy 16:11 appears again in Deuteronomy 26:11–13, where the migrants and others once more share in the bounty of the community as it celebrates its life together under God.

The homiletical framework around these groups of laws in Deuteronomy 12–26 also refers to the legal status of migrants. A parade of the relevant texts perhaps illustrates the depth of Deuteronomy's commitment to their protection:

> I [i.e., Moses] commanded your judges at that time, "Listen to both sides of a dispute among your brothers and judge fairly between each one and his brothers or his *ger*." (Deut. 1:16)

> For Yahweh your God is a God of Gods and Lord of Lords, the great and mighty and awe-inspiring God who does not show favoritism or take a bribe, the one doing justice for the orphan and widow, and loving the *ger* to give that person food and clothing. So you should love the *ger* since you were *gerim* in Egypt's land. (Deut. 10:17–19)

> All of you are standing before Yahweh your God . . . your babies, your wives, and your *ger*. (Deut. 29:9–10).

> Assemble the people, the men, women, babies, and your *ger* in your gates so they may listen and learn and honor Yahweh your God and pay close attention to all the words of this Torah. (Deut. 31:12)[8]

In each case, the *gerim* join native-born Israelites in the community's religious, economic, and social life.

In considering these texts, we deal with the issue of how to interpret law. Every legal system depends on procedures and personnel for translating values into laws and laws into practices. Interpretation occurs all the time, and interpreters always argue about the implications of the law. Out of that argument comes greater clarity.

Deuteronomy, therefore, focuses on the values and justifications for the values ("you were migrants in Egypt"). It also moves to specific laws that minimize abusive employment practices and reframe the relationship between native Israelite and resident alien as one of mutual support and trust. Often the text speaks of "your *ger*," parallel to "your wife" or "your Levite," as a label of personal attachment. Whatever the precise relationship between the Israelite as host and the *ger* as guest, whether one of economic dependence or partnership, Israelites bear a responsibility because of their history as a liberated people. Exploiting the migrant betrays Israel's core story and exposes the betrayer to divine judgment. Yahweh chairs the court of last resort, and Yahweh's justice works implacably.

The Stranger (*ger*) in the Ten Commandments

Other legal collections in the Pentateuch also legislate about migrants. The Ten Commandments or Decalogue, a brief, easily memorizable list of key rules that appears in both Exodus and Deuteronomy, contains an instruction about the Sabbath. Both versions of the Decalogue appear in their literary context as divine speech, beginning with an announcement that the lawgiving God is also the God "who brought you from Egypt's land" (Exod. 20:1-2; Deut. 5:6). Law and liberation complement each other. The two versions differ in the precise reason for rest (*shabbat* means "stoppage") one day in seven:

Because in six days Yahweh made the heavens and the earth, the sea, and everything in them, and then Yahweh rested on the seventh day, thereby blessing the Sabbath day and consecrating it. (Exod. 20:11)

You should remember that you were a slave in Egypt's land, but Yahweh your God brought you from there by a powerful hand and an extended arm. Therefore, Yahweh your God commanded you to observe the Sabbath day. (Deut. 5:15)

Though brief, each version offers rich theological reflection on the nature of work and rest. Exodus insists that meaningful human work, far from enslaving or degrading human beings, allows us to imitate Yahweh's creative activity. Structured times of rest fit into the cycle of creation, with Yahweh as a model of pious action. Deuteronomy, meanwhile, emphasizes the deliverance from degrading work (i.e., slavery). The day of "stoppage," Shabbat, reminds the community of its liberation, thereby fostering gratitude, empathy, and deeper awareness of the purposes of even the most mundane labor.

In the midst of all this appears the *ger*, the migrant, whom the community must also allow to rest (Exod. 20:10; Deut. 5:14). In both cases, the "migrant" wears the label "your migrant," indicating again a close relationship, perhaps even cohabitation. Migrants live in the Israelite neighborhoods.

Again, the Ten Commandments survive in slightly different versions. The differences reflect different literary contexts, with Deuteronomy's version matching closely the theology of the rest of that book, and Exodus's more closely fitting the theological concerns that appear throughout most of Exodus 25–40, Leviticus, and parts of Numbers and Genesis. Before turning to that larger unit, however, we should note one further point.

Neither Exodus nor Deuteronomy presents the Decalogue as a part of law more special than other parts. True, its "thou shalt not" (apodictic) law comes across as absolute statements, whereas other "if . . . then" (casuistic) laws reflect the nuances of life more fully. After all, one either murders or does not, steals or does not, commits adultery or does not. Prohibitions such as these appear in many law codes from many cultures. Yet the short collection of ten does allow an Israelite, even a child, to learn some basic orientations to life such as respect for God and other people.

As part of that overall approach to human dignity, then, the Sabbath law, unparalleled in ancient Near Eastern legal traditions, reflects Israelite theology and experience in a distinctive way. And the migrant features in that distinctiveness. Everyone deserves a break from work.

The Stranger (*ger*) in Priestly Laws

While innumerable Jews and Christians have memorized the Ten Commandments, many Western Christian readers find Leviticus and even Numbers hard going. Laws in those books reflect cultural practices that lack close parallels in the secularized, technology-driven, capitalist West, unless we look well below the surface. On the other hand, since most Christians now reside in Africa and Asia, the texts continue to have an appreciative worldwide audience. Sacrifice, worrying about fungal growths, and other practices seem more closely connected to personal experience.

Even for Westerners, however, it is possible to understand these texts and their preoccupations with a little effort. The principal concerns of these texts lie first with establishing the proper worship of Yahweh around the sacrificial system and then the extension of the main interest of that system, the purity of the world and its inhabitants, to everyday life. The very expansive concept of *purity*, which appears in all cultures in one guise or another, extends into the spheres of family, business, and even diet. Whatever the precise historical relationship of Deuteronomy and Leviticus, some development has occurred between them as they deal with slightly different historical realities. Hence their minor differences.[9]

In focusing on the laws revolving around the priesthood and the purity of Israel as found in Leviticus and beyond, we see two large categories of laws that stick out. First, several texts open the door to *gerim* to participate in communal worship. For example, Leviticus 16:29 asks "the migrant sojourning among you" to observe the new moon celebration (a minor festival). Several texts permit migrants to sacrifice to Yahweh on the same terms as Israelites (and therefore for the same reasons). So Leviticus 17 collects five laws inviting both those from "the house of Israel" and the *gerim* to make offerings to God and also to eat meat in appropriate ways (cf. Lev. 22:18). Here the latter are not Israelites, but foreigners closely identified with Israelite culture. Either group may eat meat properly slaughtered (i.e., drained of blood), even if not in a sacrificial environment. But Leviticus does alter one feature of the food laws of Deuteronomy, for whereas Deuteronomy 14:21 allows a non-Israelite to eat an animal that died on its own, Leviticus 17:15 prohibits such a contribution to the food supply, in part because of Leviticus's elevated interest in ritual purity for everyone, not just the priests (see also Lev. 18:26), and in part because this book conceives of the relationship between Israelites and *gerim* as more intimate. Times have changed, and the law changes to recognize closer relationships.[10]

Second, several laws deal with economic matters. The old idea of leaving the corner of the field or olive grove for the poor to pick (Deut. 24:19-22) appears again in Leviticus 23:22 and extends to vineyards as well (Lev. 19:10). More interestingly perhaps, *gerim* may take long-term leases on land, though the lease must end at the year of Jubilee, which Leviticus calls upon Israel to celebrate every fiftieth year by returning all real property to its original owner. Since the priestly laws conceive of all of Israel as Yahweh's personal estate and all farm holdings as belonging to God in the first instance and then to families in a subsidiary way, individuals could not permanently sell their property to Israelites or others.

Jacob Milgrom could be right to argue that the law preventing the *ger* from permanently owning property may have been pre-Israelite, since "When Abram had taken up residence as a *ger wetoshab* among the Hittite occupants of Hebron, he not only had to turn to the owner of his desired burial cave, but had to receive the permission of the ruling council of the entire city in order to buy the lot in perpetuity (Gen. 23:3–16)."[11] But the larger point is that the law in Leviticus 25 imagines non-Israelites owning Israelite property on the same terms as the Israelites themselves, even if, unlike in the case of Israelites, the property did not pass through a family line. Since, as far as we know, the Jubilee was never celebrated in ancient Israel, this law lives in an interesting space between the ideal and the real.[12] Landholding needed regulation to serve the higher goals of fashioning a holy people who could live together harmoniously. The presence of the *ger*, far from threatening that larger project, could support it.

The laws in Leviticus 25 also prohibit exacting interest from the settled migrant, again indicating that the accident of birth does not trump the solidarity possible between such a person and his or her Israelite hosts. In the economic system that Leviticus seeks to create or at least manage, interest-taking among neighbors violates the idea of shared identity, which it describes with the familial language of "brother" (the gender being less crucial than the genetic connection). The *gerim* are not siblings exactly, but they do receive the same sort of treatment.

In fact, the priestly law collection in Leviticus states the principles guiding this association between the Israelites as hosts and the *gerim* as more-or-less permanent guests. These diverse expressions include "When a migrant sojourns in your land, you will not oppress that person. The citizen and the migrant sojourning with you will be the same to you, and you will love that person like yourself, for you were migrants in Egypt's land. I am Yahweh your God" (Lev. 19:33–34). That is, the law accepts the Covenant Code's emphasis on the experience in Egypt as the basis for Israel's moral reflection on its own relationship as host to others (see Exod. 22:20 [English 22:21]; 23:9). Leviticus then takes that principle further by enjoining Israelites to "love" the stranger, much as they must "love" their neighbor—just as they love themselves (see Lev. 19:18).

Leviticus 19 reads a bit like a catchall of laws, with topics ranging from sorcery and divination to sex outside marriage, and unsurprisingly so, perhaps, given the range of topics a community needs to consider in fashioning its life together. All of these rules, however, attempt to turn a sentiment of respect for others into practical terms, given the realities of a certain time and place. While not all the laws make obvious sense in a modern postindustrial society, the conceptions and attitudes behind them do.

To conclude this survey of priestly law, then, one should note the appearance of laws affecting the *ger* in the book of Numbers. (Numbers includes laws on many topics similar to those in Leviticus but for some reason not placed there.) Numbers 9:14 permits the *ger* to join celebrations of the Passover (an expansion of previous laws but anticipated in Exod. 12:19, 49), and Numbers 19:10 includes them in the red heifer ritual, a ceremony for removing the pollution of sin from the community. A summary of rules for sacrifices in Numbers 15 admits the migrant to full participation, so that "there might be forgiveness [for accidental sins] for all the congregation of Israel's children and for the *ger* sojourning among you" (Num. 15:26). And the law of asylum, according to which someone who has accidentally killed another and is fearful of lynch law or the family feud may flee to a designated city, includes the migrant (Num. 35:15; similarly, Josh. 20:9). Such a person would need special protection in a society in which the long arm of the state could not always reach into the village.

Conclusions: Law and the Culture of Law

To summarize this brief survey of biblical laws about the migrants, a few things seem clear.

- Migrants enjoy under law most of the same rights as Israelites. The *gerim* may participate in a lawsuit and expect judgment to be rendered fairly. While biblical law never spells out procedures for the law court itself, the giving and taking of testimony, rules for evidence, or the conduct of judges, all these factors should work toward giving everyone access to the same justice. Hence the prohibition of bribery, influence peddling, and intimidation.

- They may participate fully in ritual life, including holidays and sacrifices, without of course holding a priestly office.
- They should avoid idolatry and worship Yahweh, just as their Israelite hosts do.
- They should obey the same food laws as Israelites, at least with respect to avoiding blood. Whether they observe *kashrut* (eat only *kosher* food) is less clear.
- Laws do not address other social markers such as art, clothing, language, or other aspects that distinguish one culture from another, indicating openness toward diversity of expression. This tolerance might explain the diversity of foreign objects found in Israelite archaeological sites from most periods of the mid-first millennium.

Perhaps other conclusions present themselves. Yet these suffice to show that Israelite law trends in the direction of openness toward migrants and away from a narrow, self-protective vision of Israel as a community. The migrant does not appear in law as a problem, but as a welcome guest that, if anything, gives the redeemed people opportunity to demonstrate their gratitude to Yahweh for the exodus and to each other their commitment to generous, ethical lives. The sort of legalism so common in modern debates about migrants—"Well, they broke the law, didn't they?"—has no place in Torah itself. Rather, Israelite law operates on the assumption that the law must serve to protect the vulnerable from the strong, as well as to call upon the strong themselves to mature in their attitudes toward others. One should ask not merely what the law says but whether its content and application fit the parameters of justice.

6 - 3

18

5 - 2 - 2

15 16 17

CHAPTER 7

The Voice of Prophecy

THE CONTENT AND APPLICATION of the law matter, not merely its formal existence.[1] All the stories and laws discussed in the previous few chapters have made several things clear. First, Israel cared about its own dual status as both a migratory people and a host of other migrants. One side of life implied the other. Second, the creators of the Bible thought, and thought that God thought, that the humanity of the immigrant trumped narrow national self-interest, much less the unsavory human passions of greed, fear, and the continuous search for an enemy to defeat. Third, migrants can exercise moral agency, not remaining mere victims of forces larger than themselves.

I picked up a story of such moral agency a few years ago in a cab ride across Los Angeles from LAX to Malibu, where I was to give a talk at a university. My driver came from El Salvador, a country that has adopted the US dollar as its currency and receives almost one-sixth of its Gross Domestic Product as remittances from its citizens working abroad. He talked about how he had come to the United States a number of years earlier to find work. Now he saved his money to send home to his wife and young son so they could have a better life. "Do you have any children?" he asked. "Two," I replied. "Let me tell you about my boy," was his proud response, one father to another. I asked him how he felt about recent political maneuvers that might affect his right to work. "I try not to be afraid. My son needs me not to be afraid." I hope he still lives that way.

If Israelite law tries to limit common human attitudes of fear of the outsider and the desire to protect one's own from them, the biblical prophetic texts take the role of migrant in a different direction. The book of Jeremiah, in particular, considers less the role of host than the status of migrants themselves. It thus presents the other side of the biblical approach, a tough-minded yet gracious wrestling with what it means to be not the host, but the one hosted.

The reality of diaspora, of being a community scattered across several countries yet still in communication across boundaries, began for the Israelites during the sixth century BCE. It still continues. This ongoing experience provided an occasion for theological reflection as prophets and poets articulated understandings of the people's new forms of life. For the sixth-century prophets and their followers, especially the circles around Jeremiah, the new realities included the end of political independence and the dislocation of previous patterns of economic and social life. They also included the separation of previously connected groups, with Israelites residing across the Near East. In response to that fact, Jeremiah sought to establish connections between the homeland and the deportees. This communication appears in a book addressed to residents of the environs of Jerusalem, but the appearance there simply reinforces the idea that Israel should remain one community, in spite of the strains of migration.

In particular, Jeremiah 29:1-32 contains summaries of two letters that the prophet sent in the diplomatic bag to the deportees to Babylonia sometime between 597 and 586 BCE, before Zedekiah's ill-fated rebellion against Babylonian rule. The Babylonian Empire had replaced Assyria but had carried on the older state's practice of deporting whole peoples. Among the deportees were citizens of Judah, Jeremiah's own people.

The prophetic text explores the problem of forced migration and the needs of the deported community to survive as a whole, not just as individuals eking out a living in a strange land. Unlike the authors of the poignant lament Psalm 137 ("by the rivers of Babylon we sat and wept when we remembered Zion") or the harrowing book of Lamentations ("Yahweh was like an enemy"), Jeremiah casts a vision of a believable future for the migrants outside their own land. He (and the book bearing his name) seeks to preserve a diaspora community's capacity for receiving, cultivating, and transmitting theological and moral knowledge.

Jeremiah 29 consists of six units described as parts of the original document sent to Babylonia, along with a seventh unit mentioning a second missive addressing the particular problem of prophetic speech at variance with Jeremiah's message that doom must precede deliverance.[2] While the material does not seem to be the transcript of the letters, there are traces of letter-writing conventions throughout the chapter.[3] Both Jeremiah and his disciples, who finished the book, sought to connect the fate of the successive waves of deportees from Judah with that of those who remained behind.[4]

After the introduction in verses 1–3, each unit begins with the oracular announcement "Thus says Yahweh," which serves both a literary purpose of demarcating the units (vv. 4–7, 8–9, 10–15, 16–20, 21–23, 24–32) and a rhetorical purpose of grounding the content of each section in the will of the deity. God has decreed a meaningful new life even in a state of dislocation. Thus the text addresses several principal concerns. These include the fate of the migrants, the roles of prophetic speech and the problems of assessing its validity, the proper understanding of the work of Yahweh in history, especially with respect to the tragic encounter with the Mesopotamian empires, and (implicitly) the ways in which the writing and circulation of texts about life in diaspora could revitalize prophetic speech beyond its original sphere of influence. Two of these otherwise interesting topics contribute especially to a Christian theology of immigration rooted in Scripture: the commitments that immigrants should undertake to build a viable life in their new lands, and the ways in which such migration might be part of the gracious work of God in the world. Let us consider each element in turn.

The Commitment to *Shalom*

As a foundational consideration, the pragmatic issues of life build-ing appear as the first oracle of Jeremiah's letter. The prophet writes,

> Thus says Yahweh of Hosts, Israel's God, to all the deportees that I deported from Jerusalem to Babylon: "Build houses and take up residence. Plant gardens and eat their fruit. Take wives and give birth to sons and daughters, and take wives for your sons and give your daughters to men. Then those women shall give birth to sons and daughters. Multiply there, and do not decrease. Moreover, seek the welfare (*shalom*) of the city to which I have deported you and pray for it to Yahweh. For in its welfare is your welfare." (Jer. 29:4–7)

This text has become so familiar that it is easy to forget its truly revolutionary nature. Although both the Neo-Assyrian and Neo-Babylonian empires resorted to mass deportations as instruments of policy from the eighth through the sixth centuries BCE,[5] no theological program comparable to that of the Israelite prophetic tradition has survived from other cultures. The prophets' speeches aimed to equip their hearers with tools of resilience in their new lives.

Apparently, the combination of ethnic self-awareness, worship of the one God not restricted to a particular place, and the Israelite prophets' habit of addressing the whole people (and not just the king as in other ancient Near Eastern prophetic traditions) made possible, in Judah, an innovative way of doing theology. Prophets like Jeremiah could reframe the thinking of a people whose attach-ment to land and temple needed reworking, but not discarding, after the loss of both.

This first section of the document to the deportees consists of five elements:

- a reference to Israel's God carrying the old title of Yahweh Se-baoth ("Yahweh of the divine armies"), first used in the sanctuary at Shiloh, and the more pertinent, or rather rhetorically potent, title "Israel's God"

- the designation of the recipients as "the deportees whom Yahweh has deported," a label that simultaneously shifts the focus from the conquerors' political analysis (according to which the gods of Babylon moved peoples around) toward the viewpoint of the Israelite prophetic traditions (according to which Yahweh did)
- instructions to engage in food production and house building, practices necessary for long-term sustenance of life
- commands to marry and have children (without explicitly prohibiting intermarriage with Gentiles)
- the invitation to pray

In the brief span of four verses, the prophetic speech connects ancient traditions to new realities and so equips the readers for pragmatic responses to biological and social imperatives. The letter offers a clear path to understanding Yahweh as the God of Israel's history even in its scattered state.

The last item in this list, the call to prayer, is especially striking. Jeremiah shifts the community's prayers away from curses of the enemy, seen in such anti-imperial psalms as 83, 137, and the older royal psalms (e.g., Pss. 2; 20; 21; 72), toward benediction. By claiming that "in its *shalom* is your *shalom*," the text raises the possibility that the empire at the center of which Jeremiah's audience finds itself can become a properly ordered society in which justice can prevail and human dignity can flourish, despite the suffering lying at the heart of that empire. The migrants' prayer somehow influences the transformation of their host society. The moral and spiritual responses they bring to bear through God's grace reverberate through the society.

How will this change of affairs happen? Jeremiah does not work out the details since prophetic speech ordinarily contents itself with images and emotions. But this lack of detail does not imply a lack of concreteness, for the command to reproduce and to tend the land points both to basic human needs, rooted in our nature as biological beings, and to a major strand of Israel's self-understanding. In all these texts, ordinary life carries the dignity God assigns it.[6] "Do you have children?" my driver's question, becomes a way of tying strangers together in common aspiration for the future. Migration, even of the most humiliating sort, neither strips the one moving of human dignity nor absolves him or her of responsibility for moral actions.

While no direct link exists between Jeremiah 29 and the laws in Leviticus or Numbers, all these texts assume that God cares for human beings and Israel in particular. This care comes to light in rhythms of building a fruitful life, in the work of growing food and building houses and bearing children, whether in Eden or Canaan or anywhere else. Plowing and praying, harvesting and hallelujahs all go together. *Shalom* takes shape in everyday life, even in a strange land and the hostile city at its ideological, political, and economic center.

This text moves the conversation to a different plane by envisioning a different place for the conquered, even with the empire's current social structure. Jeremiah does not believe the empire to be a permanent fixture in Yahweh's plan for Israel. Nor does he endorse every policy emanating from Nebuchadnezzar's head.

Nevertheless, this intellectual maneuvering distinguishes Jeremiah 29:1-32 from other Israelite texts that view the Babylonian and other empires as impossibly corrupt and thus ripe for collapse.[7] In asking deportees to pray for the empire, Jeremiah does not propose religious escapism—he must have been one of the least escapist human beings who ever lived! Nor does he advocate accepting the Babylonian Empire's view of the world in an ultimate sense. Rather, he empowers suffering people to see themselves as agents of *shalom*, even under threat. They have access to God, and the empire, despite its delusions of power, needs them.

Yes, the adventuresome call to prayer for the empire's real interests (in contrast to its self-declared ones) remains a singularity in Israel's prophetic books, though a related idea appears in Isaiah 44-45's belief in the Persian emperor Cyrus's special role in the divine economy and the Isaianic vision of Israel, Egypt, and Assyria as coequal partners in a renewed world (Isa. 19:16–25). Somewhat later, Zechariah similarly expects entire Gentile groups to join Israel in worshiping Yahweh (Zech. 2:11–12 [Hebrew 2:15–16]). Yet Jeremiah does something Isaiah and his successors never quite manage: he suggests practical actions that the migrants could take.

Migration as a Divine Work

Let us press the point further. Jeremiah's letter to the deportees imagines a world in which the prayers of migrants can reach the God who is blessing their host nation, even if that host nation is Babylon. In this viewpoint lies the radical nature of the prophet's command. However, Jeremiah's audience need not pray for the empire's success at dominating the world and creating ever more refugees. Rather, they seek a more elusive reality called *shalom*. That is, Jeremiah's vision of prayer both supports the Babylonian state and poses an alternative to its vision of worldwide centralization.[8] For the Judean migrants, the Israelite people's center in the promised land contrasts with the empire's centeredness in Babylonia, thus exposing the problematic, contestable nature of the whole idea of center and periphery, of civilization at home and barbarism abroad. Jeremiah argues that human beings can escape the choice states sometimes impose on them: either support all we do or get out. Migrants can recognize a transcendent reality and by doing so can point even their captors toward it. Jeremiah thinks that the center of the world lies wherever a community remembers to pray to Yahweh. There lies *shalom*.

In truth, the book of Jeremiah itself offers a profile of this life of *shalom*. The word appears in the book twenty-five or twenty-six times,[9] in several literary strata, and in several ways. Sometimes peace is the elusive quality antithetical to violence or social anxiety (Jer. 4:10 = 23:17; 8:15 = 14:19; 9:7; 12:5; 12:12; 30:5). More rarely, this rigorously probing book envisions *shalom*'s effects as a major factor in human history, though only through the triumph of divine mercy over human sinfulness (Jer. 33:6, 9).[10] In due time, Yahweh will give the world the gift of *shalom*, and by praying for it the diaspora community cultivates practices embodying it. Having learned the lessons of war and forced migration, they may also acquire the knowledge of peace and serve as a conduit of that knowledge between their home and host lands.

If the letter embedded in Jeremiah 29 fits into this larger theological conception, then it becomes necessary to consider exactly how the vision of *shalom* plays out. To begin to simplify a complex picture, notice that chapter 29 immediately precedes the so-called Book of Consolation in chapters 30-33, a cluster of texts that interrupts Jeremiah's otherwise dreary catalog of human errors and the tragedies that flow from them. The Book of Consolation envisions a world in which Israel's circumcised heart will allow for a healthy relationship with the covenant-making God. Yahweh aims to restore "all the families of Israel" (Jer. 31:1) as a united people, at home and abroad. Northerners and southerners, deportees and remainers, formerly righteous and formerly not so righteous will all come together.

Whatever its ultimate duration, then, the period of living scattered about the world, the diaspora, will provide spiritual resources for the homeland as well as vice versa, thus radically reordering the nature of Israelite identity. Both land and temple will remain important, but Jeremiah makes it possible to embrace both in new ways. Exile does not destroy one's identity as a member of the community. The present cannot erase the past or stifle the future.

For the followers of Jeremiah, the final compilers of the book carrying his name, neither the previous sociopolitical arrangements of two Israelite kingdoms nor the age-old polytheistic religious practices so bitterly opposed by earlier prophets such as Hosea will survive the Babylonian conquest, but the underlying identity of Israel as Yahweh's people will continue.[11]

Perhaps the clearest expression of the new *shalom* that awaits the restored people appears in an oracle in Jeremiah 33:4-9, which reads,

For thus says Yahweh Israel's God about the houses of this city and the houses of the kings of Judah which are demolished[12]. . .

the places to which the Chaldeans come to slaughter so as to fill them with human corpses, "which I cut off in my fierce anger, and from which I hid my face"—from this city—because of all their evil. I am bringing up for it health and healing, and I will heal them. Then I will reveal for them a crown of *shalom* and trustworthiness. Moreover, I will turn the turning of Israel and rebuild them as before. I will purify them from their every transgression, which they sinned against me. And I will forgive all their transgressions that they sinned against me, by which they rebelled against me. Then this act will earn me a reputation for rejoicing, prayer, and adornment among all the earth's peoples who hear about all the good I am doing for them. And they will stiffen up and tremble because of all the *shalom* that I am doing for it.

This oracle, which comes from a later period in the book's development and reflects the final destruction of Jerusalem and surrounding regions by the Babylonians in the invasion of 586 BCE, expects a new status for the people based on divine forgiveness.[13] There has been a "turning away" from the land, but there will soon be a "turning of the turning," to use the colorful Hebrew expression *shub 'et-shebut* that indicates a reversal of the reversal of fortune.[14] The prophetic speech anticipates a new reality that will both resemble and differ from the prior reality. That is, the divinely provided preconditions of a life of integrity and well-being (e.g., the fertility of the land, safety from hostile powers) will return, while the moral response of the community and individuals within it will improve.

Memory and Identity

Throughout these texts appears a curious understanding of the prophetic word in history. Jeremiah simultaneously criticizes other prophets for predicting *shalom* when, in fact, Yahweh has decreed a time of destruction (Jer. 14:13; 28:9; cf. Jer. 38:4) and, at the same time, he announces the arrival of *shalom* in its own good time.[15]

In short, the book's understanding of *shalom* is intertwined with its theory of history, according to which a time of cultural meltdown (i.e., the so-called Babylonian Exile) must precede a time of renewal. Timing matters.[16]

A number of lessons offer themselves to the readers of these texts, then:

- Israel's experience of exile taught it the possibilities of God's presence everywhere. Yahweh came to be seen as the God of all the world, not just of one land.
- This viewpoint stimulated resources for a theological understanding of diaspora that brought the nature of communal identity to the fore so that it must be carefully considered by Jews, not just tacitly assumed.
- On a related point, no one should accept unquestioningly the state's definition of the value of the person. A deeper identity must be in play if the person is to be credited as a human being rather than an object of state violence or beneficence. No matter what the Babylonians might say, Israelites possessed a dignity transcending both their own sinfulness and other humans' assessment of them.

This theologically oriented identity emerges when a community rediscovers its past as well as the pasts of others, valuing both as windows onto deeper truths. Identity formation occurs when a community understands its own past as a presupposition for its present rather than a negation of it. For the audience of Jeremiah's letter, or the book in which it was eventually embedded, the past was one of both doom and hope, both the tragic failure of a grand dream and the revival of the dream in a better world freed from idolatry and other forms of self-deception. The vision of the past and the present as part of a single, continuous story came into focus after the fierce trial of the Babylonian invasion and deportation.

The power of such a dream for the future depends on the community's ability to remember its past or to reenact it in storytelling, ritual, and moral reflection. Judeans in the generations after Jeremiah certainly engaged in such activities, as is clear from the mentions of commemorative fasts in Zechariah (Zech. 7:1-7; 8:18-19) and the impressive intellectual project we call the Deuteronomistic History (Joshua-2 Kings), a work that sought to salvage from the past a sense of order, and therefore justice, in history.[17] Evidence for Jewish behavior in diaspora during this early period is much more difficult to come by, though we do know that Judean communities existed in both Egypt and Babylonia, and later texts such as Tobit and Esther show pious Jews even further afield (see chap. 8). Moreover, recently discovered cuneiform texts from various locales in southern Babylonia demonstrate the existence of a vigorous community of Judean exiles during the sixth and fifth centuries BCE, with individuals engaging in agriculture and other professions.[18] So there is no reason to doubt that at least some of his hearers followed Jeremiah's advice and learned to flourish as migrants in their new homes while praying to Yahweh, their ancestral God, and following the Torah as it emerged in the early Persian period.

How did they do so? At this point, we could borrow an idea from studies of historical understandings articulated by other communities. In her ethnography of union activists in Argentina, Sian Lazar argues that her subjects operated with a dual conception of time in which "'Historical time' is a sense of emplacement within a historical narrative of political action that looks back to the past and to illustrious ancestors and forwards to an imagined set of possibilities for the future; 'attritional time' is one of constant protest or negotiation, the continuance of the day to day of political life when there is no resolution in sight to a particular conflict or problem, coupled occasionally with a dramatization of what can become quite banal over time."[19]

Lazar says that we need to rethink the meaning of the label "event." An event is not just an objective reality that happened to certain persons in a certain space at a certain time. It is that, of course, but an event also plays a role in a community's overall mental picture of the past in ways that preserve and enhance that event's centrality in the community's ongoing narrative. Some things we keep remembering with intensity and others we do not. We become what we remember.

This approach to history seems fruitful for understanding Jeremiah's efforts at helping a diaspora community rethink the turbulence of its immediate past. Movement, however painful, is not just tragedy. It can provide opportunity. Therefore, the book of Jeremiah challenges a popular conception of the present as disaster and past as glorious by emphasizing the constant strife of the period just before the forced migrations and proposing the possibility of *shalom* in the empire. In other words, the Jeremiah tradition seeks a radical solution to the Judean community's oscillation between despair and wishful thinking.

Such a renegotiation of the past should not surprise anyone familiar with contemporary migration. In many diasporic communities, the first generation's reconstructed memories of the homeland's ways exist in profound tension with the second generation's loss of memory, its forgetfulness of the old place and desire to fit in with the new. Often the government of the host society compels migrants to keep detailed records of their lives, bending memory in ways that both reinforce the migrants' otherness and allow the state to pretend that its own memories somehow trump those of the migrant community.[20] Intermarriage, new language acquisition, employment patterns, and other cultural markers become contested as these communities continue in their receptor cultures.

This fraying of communal memory reflects an aspect of the nature of memory as an activity. As the philosopher Paul Ricoeur has observed, "Regardless of the ultimate destiny of the memory of dates and places on the level of historical knowledge, what primordially legitimizes the disengagement of space and time from their objectified forms is the tie linking corporeal memory to the memory of places. In this regard, the body constitutes the primordial place, the here in relation to which all other places are there."[21] He makes this point in the context of a sustained discussion of the relationship between memory as habit and memory as activity, which he seeks to map onto the idea of body as habit and body as event, demonstrating both the nature of memory as something the body does and the necessity of linking the individual mind and its memory functions with the world outside it.

Memory is negotiable, but a process of negotiation always implies a set of rules and coequal partners, not the arbitrary act of one person. For migrants in particular, the disconnection between body and space—the removal of bodies from the spaces in which they previously belonged—creates a problem for memory as habit as well as both a challenge and an opportunity for memory as practice. The migrant community must cultivate (hence shape and even distort) its communal memory of "home" if it wishes to survive.

If, then, we combine Lazar's emphasis on temporality alongside spatiality (when as well as where something happened) with Ricoeur's notions of memory, we arrive at an idea that seems theologically fruitful. A community, in order to remember its place of origin, must maintain some sort of tie in the form of bodily practice, sometimes in the form of dress or food-consumption patterns, but also in the bodily practices of spirituality. Otherwise the community dies. Hence, Jeremiah's emphasis on precisely these elements. He was seeking to preserve the community's identity by reconfiguring its conception of time.

To put his views clearly, "we got here (Babylon) but must remember there (our homeland) so that wherever we find ourselves, we can remember that God has always lived with us and sought good for us." That trick of memory requires imagination, which the prophet seeks to cultivate not just through words, but through a set of everyday, easily understandable and replicable practices. The migrant must survive by remembering and imagining.

The Divine Origins of Human Dignity

To summarize ideas so far, then, in these oracles and others in the book, Jeremiah and his disciples understand the forced migrations that Israel and Judah experienced as a phase in the divine plan, a period of spiritual discipline and reform leading to a better state in which Israel lives out the covenant that Yahweh originally offered.

This fact explains, among other things, the appeal of Jeremiah to a primordial theme in the Israelite tradition, seen already in the ancient poem in Exodus 15:14–16, namely, the reputation of Yahweh among the foreign nations.[22]

However, Jeremiah 29 and 33 offer the raw materials for something more. By acknowledging the possibility of normal life outside the land of Israel, including the continuation of the worship of Yahweh, and by affirming that both those deported and those left behind remained in relationship with God, the prophetic work relativizes the experiences of migration. It no longer seems a death sentence but a problem to manage and a source of moral reflection. Those outside the promised land should be concerned for its fate, and those remaining at home should feel solidarity with those in diaspora. Perhaps most importantly, the experience of forced migration promotes a spirituality centering on the prayer for peace. Thus the text opens the door to a form of identity formation not dependent on physical presence in a location but on emotional attachment to the community that originated in it.

Opening up this space for thinking about the life of the migrant may be Jeremiah's greatest contribution to Israel's faith tradition. Jews and their Christian cousins have not abandoned a deep love for the ancestral homeland as a special site for God's mercy extended to all humanity. Yet they have also come to believe that the value of human beings, either singly or in groups, cannot derive ultimately from place of birth or mode of life. The state does not get to decide what a human being is in the final analysis. Rather, the state's legitimacy rests on how it treats those human beings who must move about. Migrants owe the state their prayers, but not necessarily their love or even their obedience. Jeremiah's seemingly naive call to prayer proves to be an astute reclaiming of the displaced person's place in a divine work of rehabilitating people and their systems.

CHAPTER 8

Israel as Migrant
and Host of Migrants

W E ALL LOOK FOR A PLACE in the world, usually by trying to understand ours in relationship to those of others. Such understanding grows slowly, often imperceptibly, until it surprises us with a new view of reality.

Or so it has been with me. Probably the first time I became aware of large-scale movements of people was in 1975 or 1976. Thousands of Vietnamese refugees, the so-called "Boat People," found a temporary home at Fort Chaffee, Arkansas, a mothballed military base just miles from my hometown. As a fifth-grader, I spent Sunday afternoons with other members of my boyhood church worshiping with those men and women. Mostly I remember gawking at them, not comprehending the forces of nature and politics that had shunted them to us in such needy circumstances. Later I learned of the US government's attempts to help resettle the thousands who had left Vietnam after the war. Perhaps we all felt a sense of obligation to former allies and a sense that Christian, or just human, mercy should extend to desperate people. Motivations elude me after so long a time.

The resettlement of Vietnamese, Cambodians, and Laotians in my hometown has transformed it in some ways. New restau-

rants and stores have sprung up, and new surnames appear in the
newspaper wedding announcements and obituaries. I eventually
befriended schoolmates from those countries, without ever learning enough about what they had seen. Maybe they also wanted to
forget, to move on, to fit in. Or maybe sharing memories comes
only in an environment of mutual trust, a hard-earned gift at all
times.

Communities came to coexist, sometimes interacting in public schools and public businesses, sometimes living parallel lives.
We whose ancestors had arrived in other boats in other centuries
acknowledged the aliens among us, but did not truly engage with
the patterns of their lives that both transformed the old ways with
new habits and a new language, and created something that was
neither Asian nor the sort of American that had existed before, but
a new thing. We encountered a diaspora.

Diaspora is a tricky word, however. A loanword from Greek
meaning "scattering" or "dispersal," it entered English about three
hundred years ago via scholars of the New Testament. They used
the word as the New Testament itself did, to describe the Jewish
communities living around the Mediterranean world but remaining in contact with each other about two thousand years ago. The
word has kept that two-sided meaning, describing a community
scattered yet interconnected. Modern scholars of immigration
sometimes like to refer to "multinational communities" to indicate
the fact that groups of migrants, forced or unforced, often live in
several nation-states while both retaining old customs and building
communication networks lacing together the home country and
new settlements. Sometimes one can map these diasporas, showing
how people move back and forth within them and even how they
may interact with other diasporas who share similar challenges.[1]

Now, modern diasporas reflect modern problems and solutions, some of which ancient people could not have experienced
because of major economic and technological differences between
our time and theirs. Yet many dimensions of their lives remain surprisingly similar to ours, and so the ancient Israelite texts about diaspora remain surprisingly fresh. These stories, poems, and visions

insist on the coexistence of old and new, here and there, original homeland and new homeland. In the collision of memory, experience, and imagination lay new opportunities for human creativity and a deeper awareness of the presence of God.

Israel in Diaspora

Collectively, these texts resist the perennial human tendency to equate any group's own cherished beliefs and practices with the desires of God. Quite the opposite. The God who liberated the immigrants lodging in Egypt held their descendants to a high standard in all their interactions with others.

This high standard appears in a number of texts from the Second Temple period (ca. 538 BCE-70 CE). Jews during this period—and we can speak of them as Jews as well as Israelites for the first time during this era—lived in several worlds. Many lived in the ancestral homeland itself, though now under foreign rule. Others lived in diaspora. Means of communication among the various communities existed, though efforts at communication must often have strained against the slowness of travel (by our standards at least) and the natural tendency of people to imitate their neighbors' clothing, language, food, and work rather than staying in touch with relatives separated by the miles. Jewish life at one end of the Persian Empire differed from Jewish life at another end. Yet the texts that survive from this period, as Erhard Gerstenberger puts it in his major history, "indicate the fundamental opening of their own closures and a readiness for co-existence."[2]

Esther as Foreigner

One of the most exciting of these texts, the book of Esther, tells the story of how a beautiful young queen preserves her people from the predations of a vengeful, conceited official named Haman and his tipsy king, Ahasuerus (known to the Greeks as Xerxes). This novella portrays life in the Persian royal court as a farce, complete with Olympic-level bouts of drinking, stupid decision-making by big-shot leaders, and clever manipulation through female wiles.

Esther is a comedy. But of course comedy can make a serious point, and here the point is that life in the Persian Empire poses dangers to the Jewish people because irresponsible leaders allow the killing of innocent people simply to satisfy petty vanity.

The exchange between Haman and Ahasuerus reveals important dynamics of life in a diaspora community as their neighbors view them: "Haman said to Ahasuerus, 'There's a certain people scattered and spread out among the people in all the provinces of your kingdom. Their laws differ from every other people's laws. Nor do they keep the king's laws, so it makes no sense to give them rest. So, if the king pleases, let an order be given to slay them, and I will allocate ten thousand talents of silver to those doing the work to bring to the king's treasury'" (Esther 3:8–9).

This short speech exhibits many of the tricks of mass murderers through the centuries. It identifies a dangerous enemy who lurks everywhere, labels their distinctive qualities ("their laws") as defective or menacing, and proposes a violent remedy topped off by an economic incentive (money flowing into and out of the royal treasury). It fails to specify the moral failures of the "enemy" and hides those of the speaker's group. Only in this way can Haman and his countless successors turn the victim into the perpetrator and the perpetrator into the victim. The gullible ruler, who apparently has never heard of the Jews, accepts his associate's claims at face value.

As the story unfolds, the arrogance of Haman and the irresponsibility of Ahasuerus flow out of a more systemic defect. Israel's laws differ from Persia's, but in the book of Esther, Persia's laws prove to be inflexible (the silly "law of the Medes and Persians," which can never be changed), oriented toward violence, and often sidetracked into straight-out pleasure seeking, as when the Persians feast "according to the law" (Esther 1:8).[3] Unlike the kings of the book of Daniel, who repent after throwing Daniel or his friends into lions' dens or superheated furnaces, Ahasuerus never admits any responsibility for the misdeeds of his reign, a point that underscores a signal fact of life in diaspora. The host state can easily avoid taking moral responsibility, even when its guilt screams out for attention. Power blinds its holders to their own ethical lapses and seduces them into a sense of omnipotence. But even in such an empire, the clever and gutsy survive.

The book of Esther was written in Hebrew in probably the fourth century BCE or a little later. It continued to grow in later editions and eventually ended up also in a Greek translation, which updated the book by tying up loose ends in the narrative and making it more religious with a few strategically placed prayers. One of the loose ends appears in Greek Esther just after the agreement to kill the Jews. Hebrew Esther says that the king issued a decree, and Greek Esther composes a decree for him to issue. In ornate language addressing, "everyone from India to Ethiopia, the 127 provinces and districts," the decree presents the king as one who rules with restraint, mercy, and wisdom, whose equally wise adviser Haman has brought to his attention a "people uniquely ill-willed" and following "strange laws" (Esther 3:13e), namely, the Jews.[4] These he now proposes to exterminate, root and branch. Danger lurks behind the pretty words.

One wonders what a town receiving such a decree would have thought as it licensed every bigot and predator to wreak havoc on a previously quiet population. In fact, the book can only prevent the destruction of the Jewish diaspora communities by having Ahasuerus at the end issue a decree allowing them to defend themselves, thus creating an accidental civil war. Comedy, yes, but of a dark sort. The folly of Gentile rulers becomes a vehicle for God's mercy, against the wishes of those rulers themselves.

It is not entirely clear how the book of Esther traveled around the ancient Near East. Its author seems to have known the royal palace in Susa (in southwest Iran) or palaces like it, or at least to have known people who did, but the book probably originated elsewhere. The translated and expanded version arrived in Egypt sometime between the 110s and 70s BCE, according to the end of the Greek book. So the book had legs, probably because it told a story of survival and resilience in diaspora. It celebrated the migrants' dignity in contrast to the host culture's utter lack of dignity.

Tobit and Ordinary Piety

Later than Esther, probably around 200 BCE, the book of Tobit tells the story of another family of Israelites deported during the late eighth-century invasions of their homeland to the other end of the Assyrian Empire.[5] They find themselves in Media, the western part of modern Iran. Tobit and his wife Anna (or Hannah) produce a son, Tobias, who in the main part of the story sets off as a young adult to find a suitable bride.

She turns out to be a beautiful Jewish girl named Sarah (what else?), a distant cousin of his. Though hailing from a good family, at once religious and prosperous, she carries an unfortunate liability. She has married seven times before, but on each wedding night a demon kills her husband before the marriage can be consummated. Warned by a traveling companion (who turns out to be the archangel Raphael) and by Sarah's own father of the danger of marrying her, Tobias proceeds anyway. Burning some homemade incense of incredibly stinky fish gall, he drives away the demon, whom Raphael can then bind up in northern Africa, far out of reach. And so Tobias consummates the marriage, returns home with his new wife, and lives happily ever after.

Just as Esther reveals more comedy than straight-up history, so too does Tobit go in for a sort of magic realism in which every mishap and chance encounter contributes to the final success of the hero and his family. Tobit, like Esther, entertains as well as instructs.

The instruction occurs in several dimensions. First, the story explores real aspects of life in diaspora, including the need to find a suitable mate, the dangers of travel to and from one's new home, and the interconnections among communities of like mind and like chromosomes. The quest for a mate hearkens back to Genesis's stories of Isaac and Rebekah, Jacob and Leah and Rachel, and perhaps others. It is a very human story since shared values and commitments make for much stronger marriages than other attractions usually do.

Second, it connects its heroes' lives, with their mixture of the mundane and the magical, to the work of God. The book does theology by telling stories, allowing its characters to explore the struggles of life in diaspora while overcoming difficulties. The reader can share their successes vicariously and imitate their commitments.

On returning home, Tobias greets his aged parents, who in turn break out in prayer. Tobit's prayer in particular sets forth a deeply nuanced religious view of life in diaspora. Among other things, he says,

> Confess God, Israel's Children, before the nations,
> For God has scattered you among them,
> But has also shown his greatness to you even there.
> So elevate God before all living things,
> Because he is our Lord and our God and our Father forever.
>
> (Tob. 13:3-4)

The prayer continues with a two-sided analysis of Israel's history as one in which God has disciplined them with deportations because of their sins but simultaneously exercised power even in the diaspora to defend them from oppressors. That is, living away from the homeland need not merely signify divine disfavor, for Israel's God exercises benevolence wherever penitent people reside.

The prayer continues with a personification of Jerusalem, addressing the city with

> Jerusalem the Holy City,
> God has disciplined the works of your hands
> And again will have mercy on your righteous children.
>
> (Tob. 13:9)[6]

Tobit's prayer continues with the fond hope that God will restore Jerusalem and allow both Jews and Gentiles to worship there, in keeping with the expectation of the prophet Isaiah (Isa. 2:2-4) and others.

That is, the book of Tobit conceives of Jews in diaspora as part of a transnational community, to use the modern buzzword. No matter where they lived, Jews could worship God, celebrate the ancient festivals and tell the ancient stories, and remain in connection with one another as well as to Jerusalem itself. In other words, major aspects of the view of Jewish life that still prevails today had already emerged by the third century BCE. That view rested on an explicitly religious foundation which understood human beings as subjects of a just and merciful God who must live together in harmony, not for abstract or obscure reasons, but for their own well-being in this world, as well as the next.

Daniel and the Crisis of the Second Century

Esther and Tobit together illustrate the range of possibilities available to Jews thinking about their status as migrants. The circulation of these books and others illustrates how interconnected various Jewish communities came to be. More influential than either, however, the book of Daniel offers a key witness to Israel's case for understanding diaspora as a place for God's mercy, as well as God's disciplinary, educational work.

The book reflects in part events of the 160s BCE, a moment of extreme crisis in Israel's life. During that period, Antiochus IV Epiphanes ruled Syria and Palestine. A member of the Seleucid dynasty that had succeeded Alexander the Great, he imposed on Jews in Jerusalem and elsewhere a series of drastic restrictions of their religious life. He sacrificed a pig on the altar in Jerusalem itself, consecrating the temple to Zeus Olympos. Not surprisingly a revolution ensued.

The book of Daniel refers to those events in its final chapters as it speaks of the rise of Alexander and his overthrow of the Persian Empire (Dan. 8:1-26). Among the colorful visions at the end of the book comes a description of one of Alexander's successors, who turns out to be Antiochus Epiphanes. This king invaded Egypt only to be faced down by the Romans (the "Kittim" in Dan. 11:30), after which he dispatched to Jerusalem "forces" that "stood and defiled the fortified sanctuary and eliminated the daily sacrifice, replacing it with the defiling abomination" (Dan. 11:31). Antiochus erected on the altar of Yahweh a "defiling abomination" or "abomination of desolation," as older English translations put it, apparently as part of an overall program of instituting Greek religion in the land of Israel (1 Macc. 1:41–50, 54–47; 2 Macc. 6:1–6). The book of Daniel seeks to find religious sanity in the midst of such a time of crisis or in living memory of it.

Between these two highly symbolic narrations of history lies a meditation on Israel's future and a prayer for the same, both of which reveal Daniel's key understandings of what it means to live in a diasporic community. The book connects life outside the land of Israel (with Daniel and his comrades in Babylon) to that inside it (since Antiochus's machinations applied primarily to the environs of Jerusalem). It assumes that readers will show familiarity with and prayerful concern for Jewish life in both locations.

Daniel's meditation on the future draws on the text of Jeremiah, the prophet who lived during the crisis of forced migration resulting from contact with the Babylonian Empire. Daniel's biblical exegesis, in the form of a vision, concludes that the epoch of Israel's separation from its land will last not seventy years (as in Jer. 25:11–12; 29:10–14), but seventy "weeks" or clusters of seven years, that is, 490 years (Dan. 9:24). In other words, Daniel accepts the prophet Jeremiah's idea that Israelites will live among Gentiles for a long time. The later book also retains the surface level of the earlier one, but through an interpretive sleight of hand (70 really means 490 or 70 x 7), Daniel explains the experience of Jews throughout the centuries after the so-called Babylonian Exile as a continuation of it. The old ways had not returned. In some ways they never have. Acknowledging that fact freed Daniel's readers from both false hopes and unnecessary self-reproach.

Alongside this bit of complicated biblical interpretation, the book of Daniel reports a prayer by its hero. The prayer in Daniel

9:4–19 sets forth major theological themes that emerged from Jews' consideration of the witness of the earlier books of the Bible. These themes became central for later Christian reflection on diaspora as well. After an extended confession of the sins of the ancestors, especially their leaders (Dan. 9:5–6), we hear the confession "Righteousness belongs to you, O Lord, but disgrace belongs to us today, to the Judahites and Jerusalemites and all Israel, both far away and near, in all the lands to which you expelled them because of their acts of betrayal against you" (Dan. 9:7). And then the prayer returns to confession, acknowledging the thoroughgoing sinfulness of the people and the wretchedness of their fate.

Such abject confession serves several purposes, no doubt. It calls the human audience to account for their actions, stripping away all sense of self-importance, all tendencies toward self-justification or buck-passing. Penitence means taking responsibility and resuming agency on the part of the penitent person, who becomes more than a bystander in his or her own life. Confession also shifts the responsibility back to God, who must decide whether inflicting perpetual suffering on such newly self-aware people makes sense. Mercy fits the divine nature better. It is less embarrassing for all concerned.

Such a shift back to God's agency allows the prayer to conclude by asking for the deliverance of Jerusalem. The prayer calls to mind the core Israelite story by asking Yahweh,

> So now, O Lord our God, just as you brought your people from Egypt's land by a strong hand and you built your reputation up to this very day, we have sinned and done evil. Lord, in all your justice, let your anger and your wrath abate from your city Jerusalem, your holy mountain, for because of our sins and our ancestors' iniquities Jerusalem and your people fell into disgrace among all those surrounding them. But now listen, O our God, to your servant's prayer and his petitions and smile upon your defiled sanctuary, for the sake of your own name. (Dan. 9:15–17)

The prayer connects several themes: the exodus, an understanding of Israel's history as one of sin, and a deep-seated affection for Jerusalem as a symbol of the people's hopes in God (and God's hopes for the people). As in Tobit, a deportee prays for the well-being of Jerusalem, illustrating the interconnectedness of the Jewish community in diaspora.

History and Its Lessons

The centuries after the Babylonian deportations from 604–586 BCE found Israelites living both in the land of their ancestors and further afield. Jews built new communities throughout the Middle East and eastern Mediterranean, retaining their age-old connections to the center while also taking on board the experiences of their host countries. Jews in Alexandria, for example, formed a large, mostly Greek-speaking community that nevertheless held fast to Torah, honored the temple in Jerusalem, and worshiped the one God. Other communities flourished in southern Iraq, Babylonia, and Iran, the zone of the Parthian and then Sassanian Empires. Adaptability and resilience occurred not through either assimilating with the host culture or standing in absolute opposition to it. Creative engagement made that possible.

In the process of this engagement, Jews as readers of Israel's sacred Scriptures came to understand human nature in a new way. They recognized themselves as part of an imagined community, a network of people related by birth and religious commitment even amid enormous variations in practice. They learned to choose markers of identity with care. For example, Jews in Babylon could pick up local names (Daniel became Belteshazzar, and his friends Hananiah, Azariah, and Mishael became Shadrach, Meshach, and Abednego). Greek- or Latin-speaking Jews could assume names like Philo or Aquila or Paul or Peter. Jewish synagogues could follow Hellenistic architectural styles, and inside them, Jews could worship in Greek or another local language. Even the Bible itself circulated in translation. So some major aspects of the host culture could play a role in a diaspora community without the group losing its core identity.

Other features could not. Worship of the one God and commitment to major moral practices articulated in Torah became the cornerstones of Jewish identity even when the host culture opposed those beliefs and behaviors.

In short, the existence of a diaspora requires careful thinking and equally careful socialization. Knee-jerk solutions will not do. Yet this process of identity formation benefits both the hosted migrants and the migrants' host. As the Jewish thinker Jesus son of Sirach (about 200 BCE) put it, in describing Israel's most famous ancestor,

> Abraham was the father of a multitude of nations;
> He gave away none of his glory.
> He kept the commands of the Most High
> And conducted himself in his people's covenant.
> In his own flesh he cut a statute for himself,
> And in his testing, he was found loyal.
> Therefore, he was promised
> That his offspring would bless the nations. (Sir. 44:19–21)[7]

The existence of an international Jewish community presented its members with an opportunity to transmit Torah to the wider circles of humanity. Like Abraham, they could bless their host country wherever it was, for in their common destiny lay hope.

In part that destiny must rest on knowledge, values, and commitments that human beings share. By not assimilating fully to its host cultures, Jews two thousand years ago preserved a spiritual legacy of rigorous moral self-examination, suspicion of theologies that equated human desire with God's will, and trust in a God whose passion for justice and mercy embraced humankind. By nevertheless living among many cultures, Jews became the vanguard of those very ideas and values as they spread out in the larger world. Among their heirs are the early followers of a Jewish sage, Jesus of Nazareth. To that story we now turn.

CHAPTER 9

New Testament Transformations

CLEARLY, THE TEXTS JEWS WROTE under Persian and, later, Greek rule took seriously the experience of diaspora. Jews came to see themselves as part of a community crossing international boundaries and speaking both the ancestral language of Hebrew and later the more widely used Aramaic and Greek as well. They developed channels of communication that allowed the transfer of people, texts, ideas, and practices across large parts of the Mediterranean world.

Sometimes Jews faced open hostility from their neighbors. Sometimes they felt at home. Yet in varying circumstances a new self-understanding arose as they saw themselves as both residents of a particular place and as members of a group united by loyalty to the one God and God's ongoing relationship with them.

Far from pushing Israelites further into nationalistic self-promotion, the texts preserved in the Hebrew Bible or Old Testament, as well as slightly later texts outside that collection, encouraged a stance of confidence toward the world. This confidence also fostered a habit of care for the migrant and openness to the outsider. It allowed synagogues around the eastern Mediterranean to accept

Gentile converts who embraced worship of the one God and the moral commitments flowing from Torah. It also sustained Jews when the prejudices of their neighbors turned violent, as they did from time to time.

The first followers of Jesus of Nazareth inherited such an attitude and extended it even further.[1] Perhaps the most important shift in the church's first century came when it opened the door to Gentiles. The newcomers did not at first displace Jews or Jewish practices, but entered into an equal partnership in which the boundaries between insider and outsider, between heirs of God's longstanding promises and descendants of straight-up pagans worshiped and served side by side. Without romanticizing the early church, which had its problems, as the New Testament testifies, we should recognize the extraordinary social innovation that the early Christians carried out, or, as they would insist, that God carried out.

They did so in the context of the early Roman Empire, a political structure that engulfed territory now divided among three-dozen countries. By the time of Jesus's death, the empire had existed for decades and would survive for centuries more, creating a sense of permanence and almost divinely decreed inevitability. The empire's survival depended on political skill, economic interaction, and the ever-present threat of brute force. Yet amid that multicultural state based on military power lived the small band of Christians, a multicultural community based on shared belief and mutual love.

The New Testament often addresses the church's place in the empire, whose claims to permanence and divine sanction the early Christians doubted and whose often violent attempts at bringing meaning to subjects' lives they resisted. Christians lived on the basis of a view of humanity that took diversity as an expression of God's mercy and creativity, a reality anticipating the overcoming of death and the knitting together of all humanity in the heavenly kingdom.

To make sense of its life in this world, the church from its earliest decades identified itself as a migrant community. They adopted the Old Testament's view that hosts and visitors owed something to each other. Their mutually supportive relationship said something important about the nature of human existence before God.

As the epistle to the Hebrews put it late in the first century CE, the exemplary ancestors whom the church imitated "all died according to faith, not having received the promised things, but having seen and greeted them a long way off, and acknowledging that they were aliens and migrants in the land" (Heb. 11:13). A few decades later, toward the end of the second century, the apology for Christianity known as the "Epistle to Diognetus" spoke in a rhetorically hard-hitting way of the self-contradictory status of Christians as "living in their own countries, but as sojourners, doing their part as citizens but remaining aliens in every circumstance—every strange country is theirs, and every country is yet strange."[2] A two-sided life makes for a healthy community.

At times, the church's identity as a voluntary, cross-cultural community not based on coercion cost Christians dearly as they struggled for safety in their native cities, especially when demagogues or even high officials turned their strangeness against them in order to curry favor with mobs. At other times, the sense of being both located and on the move fostered spiritual growth and intellectual creativity in new circumstances. This was the story of the church during much of its early history. In many parts of the world it still is.

The early Christians' self-conception owed much to both their own experiences and the Scriptures they shared with Jews. As it moved, the church accumulated new ideas, new experiences, new ways of being. It presented itself as a body whose suspiciously nonsedentary character demonstrated its value, not its threat, to the orderly world that inhabitants of the Roman Empire valued.

Jesus as Stranger and Host of Strangers

When early Christians presented their message to inquiring Roman subjects, they did so in several media, especially in the form
of stories. Most crucially, they recounted Jesus's interactions with
disciples, interested listeners, and sometimes adversaries. In their
reports about Jesus and his first followers, they also narrated their
own lives as they sought to imitate Jesus in some way.

Today we encounter the earliest Christian preaching about Jesus's words and deeds only through the texts that survive, especially
the four Gospels, written near the end of the first century.[3] Drawing on older material, these texts attempted to formalize Christian
teaching about Jesus, to bring some clarity to the confusion that
anyone who has spent much time in church knows can exist whenever people talk about their most cherished ideas.

So what do the Gospels say about Jesus and the migrant or
stranger? For one thing, they both adopt the vocabulary of the
Greek Bible and innovate new language to talk about the issues
around migration. They adapt to new realities.

When Jews translated the Pentateuch, Prophets, and Writings from Hebrew and Aramaic into Greek from the third century BCE onward, they ordinarily translated the Hebrew word
ger with a coinage of their own, *prosēlytos*.[4] Greek had already
given them the word *epēlytos* ("foreigner"), which they could
modify by adding a different preposition, a common enough pro-
cedure in the formation of Greek words.[5] The new word *prosēlytos* came eventually to mean "convert," and in later rabbinic texts
written in Hebrew or Aramaic, the word *ger* also took on that
same meaning.

Tellingly, the New Testament writings studiously avoid the
word *prosēlytos* except when referring to Gentiles who hang out at
the synagogue but have not (yet) embraced the teachings of Jesus
(Matt. 23:15; Acts 2:10; 13:43). The New Testament writings do use
other words for "migrant," especially when quoting Greek translations of the Old Testament that already use those words. We will
come to that point momentarily.

Now, vocabulary never tells the whole story. But it is instructive that the early followers of Jesus are more likely to cite him using the Greek word *xenos* ("stranger"), a word that the Greek Bible sometimes uses to translate *ger* (Job 31:32), but more often as the gloss for the Hebrew word *nokri*, a foreigner who does not yet enjoy an intimate relationship with the Israelite community or an Israelite outside his or her habitat.[6] The *xenos* has migrated from a familiar place to one in which the locals must greet him or her as a stranger.

In the Gospel of Matthew, Jesus makes clear his and his followers' status as the *xenos*. At the Last Judgment, as Matthew's Jesus puts it, "The king will say to those on his right, 'Come on, you who are blessed by my father. Inherit the kingdom prepared for you from the formation of the world. I was hungry and you fed me, thirsty and you gave me a drink, a *xenos* and you housed me, naked and you clothed me, sick and you nursed me, in prison and you came to me'" (Matt. 25:34–36). Astonished, the righteous question the royal judgment, which they find to be undeserved, since they have apparently struggled to live up to such an ideal. Equally astonished are the self-appointed righteous, the spiritual show-offs, who hear a few lines later that neglecting such basic acts of generosity to vulnerable people cancels out their self-promoting exercise of flashy spiritual gifts such as prophecy and exorcism. The king at the final judgment has obviously not consulted human beings in deciding on what constitutes religious success.

What does Matthew aim at in this text? In the first place, his portrayal of Jesus does not reject Judaism, for the care of hungry, impoverished people lay at the center of Jewish moral thinking. Hospitality toward Jews visiting a town was a given throughout the Roman Empire, a fact that explains much of the Apostle Paul's behavior in the book of Acts, to take just one example. Every synagogue of any size doubled as a clearing house for Jewish travelers needing a room or a hot meal. Jesus offers nothing new on that front when he expects his followers to help vulnerable people.

He does emphasize, however, his own status as the hungry, thirsty, naked, homeless migrant. That is new. A king who comes to the unsuspecting disciples as a beggar is an odd sort of king. A disciple who cannot remember his or her own acts of generosity is an odd sort of disciple. And a text that insists that the world leans in the direction of just those people is an odd sort of text. Yet the story of the Last Judgment in Matthew 25 offers just such a bundle of oddness. Matthew insists, or rather says that Jesus insists, that the community following the Messiah must embrace its own dual role as both stranger and host of strangers. "When you did it to the least of these my siblings, you did it to me" marks the church out as the community of those by turns needing and offering help.

Indeed, a broader look at the traditions about Jesus confirms such a view. It is true that Jesus's own circles did not seem to include Gentiles. Some stories show him insisting that he had been sent "solely to the lost sheep of the house of Israel" (Matt. 10:6), or that "it's not right to give the children's food to the dogs" (Matt. 15:26). However, they also show him accepting a Gentile woman's clever retort, "Yes, but even dogs eat the scraps that fall from the table" (Matt. 15:27) and anticipating that some of "the kingdom's children will be cast into darkness" while some Gentiles join the heavenly banquet (Matt. 8:11–12). The stories never speak of him entering the rising Roman metropolis of Caesarea or attending the theaters of Romanized Palestinian cities, but they do show him interacting with Gentiles in respectful ways when necessary. In other words, Jesus comes off in the Gospels as a very religious Jew, the victim of Roman occupation rather than one enjoying its pleasures.

At the same time, a few stories do place him in connection with Gentiles, even Roman soldiers. To take a key example, Matthew 8:5–13 and Luke 7:1–10 tell two slightly different versions of the same story.

When he [Jesus] got to Capernaum, a centurion approached him with a request: "Sir, my servant is stove-up in my house, in excruciating pain." So he replied, "I will go heal him." But the centurion responded, "Sir, I don't deserve for you to come under my roof. Just say the word, and my servant will be healed. I am also a man who follows orders and has soldiers under him. I say to my slave 'go' and he goes, 'come' and he comes, 'do this' and he does it." When Jesus heard that, he was astonished and said to his followers, "I am telling you for sure that I've never seen greater faith than this in Israel. And I tell you that people will come from the east and the west to dine with Abraham and Isaac and Jacob in heaven's kingdom. But the kingdom's children will be banished to the outermost darkness. There will be howling and teeth grinding there." Then Jesus said to the centurion, "Go on. Whatever you have sought will be given to you." And the servant was healed that very hour. (MATT. 8:5–13)

When he had finished his words so the people could hear, he went to Capernaum. A certain centurion's servant, who was dear to him, was ill and at death's door. Upon hearing about Jesus, he sent elders of the Jews to him to ask him to save his servant. They encouraged Jesus to come quickly and told him, "He deserves for you to do this, for he loves our people and built the synagogue for us." So Jesus went with them. When he was not far off, the centurion sent some friends to say, "Sir, don't bother. I don't deserve for you to come under my roof. I am not important enough for you to come. But speak the word, and my servant will be healed. I am a man who follows orders and has soldiers under me. And I say to this one, 'go' and he goes, and to another, 'come' and he comes, and to my slave 'do this' and he does it." When Jesus heard these things, he was astonished and turned to the crowd following him. He said, "I tell you, I haven't found such faith in Israel." When the messengers returned to the house, they found the slave healed. (LUKE 7:1–10)

The two stories differ in a few minor respects. In particular, Luke introduces a third party, the town elders, who can testify to the piety of the centurion. In other words, not all Roman soldiers come across as men on the make, using their power to enrich themselves or gratify a sadistic streak. Matthew lacks that detail, in part because it does not take the same pains Luke does to highlight positive experiences with the imperial authorities. But the stories make similar moves otherwise.

In both versions, sickness triggers the story. A servant falls deathly ill and can find healing only through the intervention of his soldier master. Upon contacting Jesus, either directly or through intermediaries, the centurion engages in a conversation about his own unfitness to receive the divine mercy demonstrated by Jesus. "I know how this works," the soldier seems to say. "I'm caught up in a system where I both give and take orders. But I try to be responsible, as best I can. I know real power when I see it."[7] And Jesus accredits that hardheaded analysis of the centurion by calling it extraordinary faith.

Matthew's version of the story adds a disturbing coda to Jesus's note of approval. The heavenly banquet, he says, will include the great ancestors of the Jewish people and of course many of their descendants. But not all. And it will include Gentiles as well. Matthew's Jesus foreshadows the church's eventual inclusion of both Jews and Gentiles and ties that hope to the old promises of God's gracious reception of Gentiles (see, e.g., Isa. 2:2–4; cf. Isa. 25:6–10). Faith can cut across all sorts of boundaries, it would seem.

The story of the centurion astounds anyone who thinks about it because it bends the pairing of host and guest to the breaking point. The soldier has migrated to the land of Israel as part of the army of a colonial power. He could hardly have imagined himself, at first, as a welcome guest to whom the locals owed generous support. The occupying army always stood just at the edge of becoming a predatory force, hence Jesus's commands to the soldiers to restrain themselves (Luke 3:14). But this soldier had, at least in Luke's version, opted for a different approach to his unwilling hosts. He had internalized at least some of their highest values in his own life. Even Matthew's version assumes that the centurion had followed Jesus's career with enough appreciation to take a chance on his healing capacities.

In truth, the story in both versions reminds the reader to exercise caution in drawing sharp lines between oppressor and oppressed, since in many cases a person in one camp can move to the other and back again. To take an extreme example, from another empire nineteen hundred years later, in her study of the Gulag Archipelago, the Soviet Union's infamous system of labor camps that featured prominently in the Stalinist era's murder of perhaps 20 million Soviet citizens, Anne Applebaum showed that "in the early 1930s, it was considered perfectly normal for well-behaved prisoners to 'graduate' to the status of camp guards."[8] The reverse movement also frequently occurred. The boundary between victim and victimizer often blurs in real life. Recognizing that fact does not justify oppression or make tyrants tolerable. But it does help us understand why people act as they do.

Jesus's encounter with the centurion demonstrates the courage to exercise the role of host of the migrant under extreme circumstances. This interpretation of the story comes through most clearly in Matthew, where that official has not merited any special consideration until he expresses confidence in Jesus's ability and desire to heal. Luke's version takes the edge off things a bit by showing a deeper connection between the host and the hosted.

Still, in both cases, the story reveals the radical nature of Jesus's teachings as the early church understood it. If ever suspicion of outsiders were justified, surely this case of a centurion, a cog in the machinery of occupation, offers an opportunity. Yet Jesus assumes that his own offer to heal, his agreement to relieve suffering, extends to this fellow human being. And the early Christians embraced such a view of their responsibility to others. Jesus inverts the relationship between strength and weakness, calling his disciples to do the same. We cannot always make the centurions go away, nor can we always guarantee their virtue. Sometimes we can only acknowledge that they also legitimately love and bear a capacity to trust in God. That acknowledgment shifts power from the one with the army behind him to the one who refuses to let fear of political might define his or her stance toward the world.

The Stranger in the Earliest Churches:
Paul and His Communities

So whose story gets told by the church and why? In the Old Testament in particular, most stories about wanderers move toward the promised land, rather than away from it. However, important exceptions to this rule exist, notably the Joseph story and Esther and Daniel, and if one expands the canon to include the Greek Old Testament, then Tobit would be added to the list. The New Testament extends the list still further, with Acts of the Apostles addressing both forced and voluntary Christian migration, and perhaps some of the letters including migrants among their mixed Jew-Gentile audiences.

Early Christianity treasured memories of its founding figures, the apostles, as intentional migrants who traveled as far as India to carry the gospel to an international audience. The most famous of these social entrepreneurs, the Apostle Paul, moved about the eastern Mediterranean, wearing out his sandals on the Roman road system. His reclamation of narratives of movement appears in such texts as 1 Corinthians 10:1-7, an extended meditation on Exodus, especially Exodus 14 and 32:

> I do not wish you to be ignorant, brothers and sisters, of the fact that all our ancestors were under the cloud and all passed through the sea, and all were baptized into Moses in the cloud and in the sea. They also all ate the same spiritual food and drank the same spiritual drink. For they drank of the spiritual rock that followed them—and that rock was Christ. But God was not pleased with many of them, and so they were destroyed in the desert. But all of these things were a type for us so that we might not be subject to evil desires as some of them desired. Nor should you be idolaters as some of them were (as it is written, "the people sat down to eat and drink, and then arose to revel").

Paul inducts Gentile Christians into an essentially Jewish narrative ("our ancestors"), rethinks that narrative in light of Christian liturgical practice ("baptized"), and then uses it for moral formation ("do not be . . ."). He does not erase the Corinthians' own stories of family and city but does test their moral and spiritual congruence with the biblical story. In embracing faith in the crucified Jewish Messiah, whose death and resurrection reflect God's desire to keep age-old promises to Israel, the Corinthians had retold their own stories with new characters and a new plotline.

For Paul, storytelling was closely related to what later Christians would call the sacraments, those key practices that connect human beings to God by testifying of God's greatness and mercy. Baptism and Eucharist, the ancient sacraments, cannot concretize the church's story in the absence of the church's faithful obedience to God in the patterns of daily life. Yet they do testify either for or against the church's faithfulness to its story as a community in which local, even national, identities ultimately give way to more fundamental ones as a community practicing the presence of God.[9] As Matthew Levering has put it, "The Eucharist is a 'school' of charity; it builds the Church by enabling us to enact Christ's sacrifice with him."[10]

It is not just that baptism and Eucharist transcend the boundaries drawn by nation-states and other forms of community. I am a baptized person first and an American (or whatever) a distant second. I may not check others' legal status at the Lord's Table. More importantly, the sacraments bear witness to the *shalom* for which Jeremiah's audience, and all subsequent followers of the God of Israel, have prayed.

As one who drew heavily on Jeremiah and other prophets, Paul repudiates both idolatry and a winner-take-all approach to religion by appealing to the practice of Eucharist: "because there is one bread, we who are many are one body, for all partake of the one bread" (1 Cor. 10:17). He continues his discussion of Christian solidarity with an appeal to the Eucharist as a model for Jesus's gracious invitation to participate in the narrative of God's work that embraces both times past in the suffering of the Lord and times future in his exaltation in the eschatological kingdom (1 Cor. 11:23–26). The sacraments narrate the divine presence, thereby incorporating persons into a community that embraces them as part of the narrative of God.

Of course, Paul did not camp out on the problem of human movement, though he himself was a migrant. Yet when he argues that the Christian story takes shape in the shared sacramental life of the local congregation and in its daily work of discipleship, he is also arguing that the boundaries created by socioeconomic or political forces no longer count for much. Followers of Jesus must test other loyalties in light of the primal Christian story.

Paul tested those loyalties in his own life as he trudged from city to city, following the Roman road system across Asia Minor and Greece and eventually ending up in Rome itself, where he apparently met a martyr's death. His letters frequently refer to his and his colleagues' excursions around the empire as they overcame loyalty to place with loyalty to a gospel that should embrace all humankind. For example, the final chapter of Romans lists a group of fellow migrants, many of whom he had met in Ephesus or Corinth (Prisca and Aquila, Epaenetus) or who had gained some reputation as *apostoloi* or missionaries (the male-female pair or perhaps husband-wife team Andronicus and Junia). The parade of names speaks to Paul's sense that the church consisted of both those living in their hometowns and those not.

One might argue, of course, that Paul's lists of names at the ends of his letters can include migrating people as in Romans or locals as in 1 Corinthians or Philippians, but they do not speak of crossing national boundaries. True enough. The New Testament collection includes only books written within the Roman Empire by its subjects. However, in the first century, even being a Roman citizen meant being either born in the upper crust of Rome or holding honorary membership in that city itself. "Roman" was not yet parallel to the modern idea of "American" or "Japanese." Being a subject of the empire did not make one a citizen automatically, nor was noncitizenship a liability for employment, civic participation, or other forms of social life. The Westphalian system did not exist yet.

Paul, in any case, hailed from Tarsus and traveled to other places where he must earn his way as an outsider, and so we must not impose on him our modern conceptions of citizenship. His letters reveal a man for whom being a servant of Jesus Christ, perhaps his favorite title for himself, meant holding local loyalties loosely at best.

Several of the early letters that were early on attributed to Paul, but may come from his disciples a generation or so after his death, take his basic commitment even further. Perhaps the most gorgeous descriptions of the status of the migrant whom God has welcomed into the state of grace appear in the epistle to the Ephesians. In a passage usually cited for its reference to God's grace through faith, the epistle pitches an understanding of the church as consisting of migrant and host, much in the vein of the Old Testament texts lying behind it:

> Because at that time you were Christless, aliens from Israel's kingdom [Greek: *politeia*], and *xenoi* from the covenant marked by promise, lacking hope, godless in the world. But now, in Christ Jesus, you who were far away have drawn near in Christ's blood. For he is our peace, the one making both into one, breaking through the boundary wall separating us, the antagonism in his flesh, and nullifying the law consisting of commands and rules, so that he might create the two as one new person in himself, so bringing about peace. And he has reconciled both in one flesh to God through the cross, removing the antagonism by it. Then he has gone forth proclaiming peace to you who were far away and peace to those nearby because through him we both have received the freedom to approach the Father in one spirit. So you are no longer *xenoi* or travelers [Greek: *paroikoi*] but fellow citizens [Greek: *sympolitai*] with the holy ones and members of God's household. (Eph. 2:12-19)

This molasses-thick summary of theology points to the core Christian understanding of the work of Christ on the cross in political terms. No longer noncitizens of God's empire, Gentile Christ-followers have won access to the true imperial center, God's capital, where they can live peacefully with Jews already in close connection with the promise-making God. Far from barring outsiders, the particularities of Jewish law point to the generosity of God. And even the cross, the most terrifying marker of Roman power and the ever-present danger it posed to dissidents of any stripe, has transformed into the tool of God's reconciliation.

For now, the most important element in this rich text concerns the nature of the "stranger" (*xenos*). Verse 19 calls the readers *xenoi* ("strangers") and *paroikoi* ("travelers" or "homeless people"), the latter being a common translation in the Greek Old Testament for the Hebrew word *ger* when it referred to Israel's ancestors as migrants in Canaan.[11] For Ephesians, the church's character does not lie in national or ethnic identity. The letter does not respect the empire's claims to be the last, best focus of human endeavors. It does not believe the Roman claims that peace must come to the world through the instruments of rule imperial, the *pax Romana*. Peace can only come from God, and it comes with the overthrow of the highest wall on the theological landscape, the contrast between people of promise and the godless.

Other New Testament Traditions

Other texts in the New Testament also take up the meaning of the church's existence as a multiethnic, cross-cultural community. Two examples offer special insight into the early Christian attitude.

The first occurs in the epistle to the Hebrews, already alluded to. An extended meditation, or sermon really, on Jesus as the best possible high priest, sacrifice, and temple all rolled into one, the book addresses migration in various ways. The book encourages its readers to imitate Abraham and Sarah in exercising "love of the stranger" (*philoxenia*, the opposite of *xenophobia*, or "fear of the stranger") so the church will live into its role as a home for all in tangible ways (Heb. 13:2). Hebrews reminds its readers that in exercising care for traveling strangers, some have "entertained angels without knowing." This seemingly bizarre reason, which ticks the readers' memories back to the story of Abraham and Sarah feeding angels in Genesis 18, opens up the mind-bending possibility that foreigners might ultimately carry messages from the divine realm to the human. Hostility to them risks placing one in the same boat as the Sodomians or rather in the same firestorm.

As part of its attempt to connect contemporary beneficiaries of Jesus's high-priestly intercessions to the faithful ancestors, Hebrews also reminds its readers that those folks lived in expectation of a reality they could not themselves experience. The text describes them with the vocabulary of the Greek Old Testament as *xenoi* and *parepidēmoi* as in Hebrews 11:13's "they were strangers and sojourners in the land." That line paraphrases Genesis 23:4, in which the Greek Bible translates the Hebrew *ger wetoshab* ("migrant and sojourner") as *paroikos kai parepidēmos* ("homeless person and sojourner"). Greek readers could access three words (*xenos, paroikos, parepidēmos*) where Hebrew readers had two (*ger, toshab*). So Greek Genesis, Hebrews, and Ephesians each choose two of the three possibilities available to them, but all say the same thing. The ancestors moved.

By harking back to Genesis, Hebrews turns the itinerating ancestors of Israel into the ancestors in the faith even of those who bear no biological relationship to them. Jesus's work has paved the way for the adoption of Gentiles into the story of God and thus the overcoming of older loyalties. *Overcoming* does not mean displacement. Gentiles are still Gentiles. Jews are still Jews. But a deeper identity unites them.

This deeper identity also appears in the first letter of Peter, a book as different from Hebrews as any imaginable. First Peter 1:1 addresses an audience of those "sojourning in diaspora," using the same vocabulary of *parepidēmos* as Hebrews 11:13. The audience identifies itself as a community residing away from home but still in contact with each other. The book goes on to pick up the same vocabulary of "traveler and sojourner" in 1 Peter 2:11, again insisting that its readers must conduct themselves in godly ways "among the Gentiles." Perhaps all of 1 Peter's readers were Jewish followers of Jesus or more likely a mix of Jews and Gentiles who had adopted the idea of being a community at home in many places and none.

The larger passage deserves some consideration: "Beloved, I encourage you as travelers and sojourners to avoid fleshly desires, which fight against the spirit. Conduct your lives well among the Gentiles so that even if they malign you as evildoers, they will reasonably assess good deeds and glorify God on the day of evaluation" (1 Pet. 2:11–12). This exhortation follows 1 Peter's description of the audience as those formerly "not a people, but now a people, formerly a nonrecipient of God's mercy, but now a recipient of that same mercy" (1 Pet. 2:10). Whatever their pre-Christian identity, the readers of the letter have assumed the role of the migrant who must live counterculturally with respect to basic morality.

Modern scholars assess 1 Peter differently. Shively T. J. Smith rightly interprets the book as "writing from the underclass for the underclass, not the overlord,"[12] an astute reading that allows her to hear the letter as a critique of racism in modern American life. That reading makes good sense of the text. Even more helpful, to my mind, is Paul Holloway's argument that this passage, and indeed 1 Peter as a whole, tries to equip early Christians for survival in a world where they face constant prejudice.[13] Ordering their minds, styles of communication, and ways of interacting with each other and outsiders allows the suffering Christians to survive as migrants in this mixed-up world. We can sharpen those perspectives a little by emphasizing that the readers of the book, as well as its author, perceive the church as a collection of people whose worth does not derive from living at home or fitting in with its standards and traditions. Being the other is a positive virtue from which the not-other can learn.

Redefining the Roles of Insider and Outsider

Earlier in the book we talked about the agreements that people make with one another every day in order to function. David Novak pointed us to the problem of what states do with respect to their subjects. The early Christians learned pretty quickly that migrants must realize that their hosts, who control the state, may not agree to give them the most basic shreds of human dignity. After all, Christians served a Messiah whom their state had executed as a menace to public order. The state and the various parties it responds to may fail to make reasonable accommodations for minorities or, having made those accommodations, to carry them out.

However, this sobering realization did not push Christians either to abandon their self-understanding as people on the move by pretending to fit into the dominant culture or to hunker down in fear. As the story of Jesus and the centurion reminded them, their master had opted to bless even the leaders of occupying powers. He had blurred the boundary between victim and victimizer. The early churches had opened their doors to both Jews and Gentiles, smudging the dividing lines between the God-filled and the godless and, along the way, redefining the roles of insider and outsider. Care of the stranger had become a given, a nonnegotiable aspect of Christian virtue.

What does this profile of the early church's understanding of migration mean today? Simply that no basis exists in the New Testament for Christian support of the fear of immigrants or the restrictive policies respecting them. Such xenophobia flies in the face of everything the early church stood for. To that subject we should now turn.

CHAPTER 10

A Conclusion for Now

R EACHING THE END OF A BOOK always allows the reader, as well as the author, to reflect on the journey. I have tried to discuss a range of texts in the Bible as they bear on the themes of migration, immigration, refugee status, and the various tangles of experiences that fit in this category of human experiences. The exercise aimed to bring greater clarity to those who take the Bible as Scripture about the commitments that such a belief entails. That greater clarity, in turn, should allow the church or synagogue to advocate on behalf of people on the move, whether refugees or immigrants, whatever the condition of their paperwork.

One might carry on such a learning exercise in several ways. For example, a number of studies of the Bible's views of immigrants simply content themselves with word studies of a few key terms, as though vocabulary sufficed to get at the mental picture of the texts and those who wrote them. It is easy to say, "See the Bible forbids the abuse of migrants, and therefore we must resist this or that policy." It is also easy to reply to such an approach that it has degenerated into proof-texting and special pleading. One then concludes that the Bible offers no guidance on the subject for Christians, and then often drifts into support for the brutal separation of families and other state actions that manifestly seem inconsistent with a Christian conception of human dignity. In other words, both approaches suffer from a lack of theological sophistication, though the second also carries the burden of ethical shortcoming.

An elegant summary of the latter, pseudo-Christian view appears in a Bible study presented to members of Congress by the right-wing group Capitol Ministries. Operating with an unbiblical distinction between legal and illegal immigrants and a legalism that does not coincide with the Bible's view of law, this group argues for a six-point plan:

A. Foreigners should not be allowed unregulated entry into a country. Borders and oceans should be impenetrable so as to discourage illegals entrance.

B. Foreigners should not be able to partake of any governmental entitlements. (Governments should not be in that business to begin with.) Nor should they be allowed to have any licenses, legal identification, or enrollment in any institutions.

C. Foreigners who can help advance the country (not detract from it) should be afforded sojourner/immigration consideration. It follows then that foreigners who are already in the country seeking citizenship should have citizen-sponsors who can testify to their past value, productivity, present character, and loyalty.

D. Foreigners should be required to pay taxes similar to those paid by citizens, both present and past due.

E. Illegal entrants, whether headed toward citizenship or expulsion, should be justly punished.

F. Not all of the responsibility of illegal immigration should be placed on the shoulders of each illegal immigrant because of the simple fact that the institution itself, the Government of the United States, has continually violated the biblical principles associated with immigration. The repeated, long term violations of the institution itself in specific regard to having fostered and prolonged illegal immigration, need to be taken into consideration in working out the problem.[1]

Not all conservative Christians who adopt a negative approach to immigration would adopt such a strong stance as this document. Its cruel, self-righteous tone makes it easy to dismiss except that the organization lists among its sponsors in Washington, DC, members of Congress and the president's cabinet, men and women who hold positions of great power as members of the United States Congress. So a bit of refutation seems in order.

One can pick around the margins and point to silly things here such as the idea of impenetrable borders (how militarized would they need to be?) and just precisely how the American government has violated biblical principles by being too tolerant. One could wonder how excluding from public school children brought to the country by their parents would benefit the larger society. Or since undocumented immigrants cannot receive any government benefits, why the statement would need to advocate against their doing so. Or we could question the emphasis on punishment and the insistence on describing human beings, made in God's image, as "illegals" pure and simple. All of these items mark the proposal as not at all serious, more the product of prejudice than of reasoned analysis of the Bible or anything else. So do the complete ignoring of such factors as the complex motives for migration, the possibility of inconsistency or injustice in the legal apparatus of the United States itself, or the implications of breaking up families with children who are citizens and parents who are not. The utter lack of empathy in such a statement should give pause to anyone reading the Bible as a religious text that speaks somehow to human life.

But I do not dwell on any of those points. Rather, I have tried to argue that once one considers the whole gamut of biblical portrayals of migration, the hard legalism of today's Religious Right seems as opposed to the biblical witness as a set of proposals can be. Contrary to many modern so-called Christian positions, the biblical texts seek to create a culture of empathy that holds citizenship in an earthly state much more lightly than more basic markers of human identity. When Christians support a public policy that lumps many immigrants together as criminals, that moves to deport even those who came here as children at their parents' behest, that breaks apart families in the name of a supposed attachment to the law, we do not uphold a biblical view. We betray it.

And when those of us who see the wrongdoing still remain silent, we betray it too. And so we must speak.

For the church, the witness of Scripture challenges us to identify ourselves as a community of migrants and their hosts. We repudiate the claims of rabid nationalism that would separate us from other human beings because of their paperwork or culture of origin. We embrace a view of human community that values moral commitments and potential for goodness rather than the claims of political allegiance. We celebrate a rule of law that deals realistically, not punitively, with the needs of immigrants and their employers and social networks in both countries of origin and host nations. And we use our own resources to aid refugees as they find new homes.

Yet the church's commitments do not simply concern itself. The followers of Jesus the King of strangers also bear witness to the state, calling upon officials to work toward policies that match the resources of the wealthy West to the profound needs of those fleeing war and famine. We must call upon governments to reverse the current trend toward excluding refugees from their borders at the precise moment when the needs of asylum have reached historic highs. We must oppose policies that would ignore economic realities both at home and abroad in the interest of demagogic promotion of hatred and fear. We must insist that politicians who would trade in prejudice never receive our votes or money, whatever other commitments they might make. We must reject the bastardized Christianity of "America First." Jesus's call to love our neighbor as ourselves precludes acceptance of the nation-state as the primary claimant of our loyalty.

In short, a careful consideration of the Bible's reflections on the life of the migrant pushes inescapably toward a much-accepting position on the relationship between the rich countries of the West, including the United States, and our fellow human beings on the move. Christians must vigorously oppose oppression disguised as reform, as the proposals from the alt-right and their evangelical collaborators have attempted to shift even the church's discourse away from its roots in Scripture toward a distortion of the ancient Christian views. Clarity and courage, care for the vulnerable, attention to our core story—in these qualities lie a more hopeful future.

Movement. Along with climate and terrain, the need for food and water and shelter, movement remains one of the constants of human existence. None of us stands still for long. For some, migration crosses space and time and involves the body. For the rest, the longest trip may take place in the human mind as we learn to think more broadly. Scripture gives us, as I have tried to argue, a map of both journeys and their numerous points of contact. Whether the church takes that journey remains a question.

Notes

Chapter 1

1. I have changed the names to protect the family's identity.

2. Theda Skocpol and Vanessa Williamson, *The Tea Party and the Remaking of Republican Conservatism* (Oxford: Oxford University Press, 2012), 200.

3. Skocpol and Williamson, *Tea Party and the Remaking of Republican Con servatism*, 200.

4. A brilliant telling of this story of religious development appears in Frances Fitzgerald, *The Evangelicals: The Struggle to Shape America* (New York: Simon and Schuster, 2017).

5. International Organization for Migration, "World Migration Report 2018," November 2017, 15, http://publications.iom.int/system/files/pdf/wmr_2018_en.pdf.

6. "World Migration Report 2018," 30. That number marked a decline from 2014's high of $596 billion, a bit more than the GDP of Taiwan.

7. As argued by Jan Lucassen and Leo Lucassen, "Migrations, Migration History, History: Old Paradigms and New Perspectives," in *Migrations, Migration History, History: Old Paradigms and New Perspectives*, ed. Jan Lucassen and Leo Lucassen (Bern: Peter Lang, 1999), 10–21.

8. UNHCR, "Statistical Yearbook 2014," 27–39, http://www.unhcr.org/en-us /statistics/country/566584fc9/unhcr-statistical-yearbook-2014-14th-edition.html. The numbers include both refugees, those who have left the country of their citizen-

ship, and internally displaced persons, those who have remained in their country's borders but live radically unsettled lives.

9. Brent A. Strawn, *The Old Testament Is Dying: A Diagnosis and Recommended Treatment* (Grand Rapids: Baker Academic, 2017).

10. International Organization for Migration, "International Migration and Development: Report of the Secretary-General," UN General Assembly, A/68/190 (July 25, 2013), 14–15.

11. David Novak, "Law: Religious or Secular?" in *Tradition in the Public Square: A David Novak Reader*, ed. Randi Rashkover and Martin Kavka (Grand Rapids: Eerdmans, 2008), 177.

12. Novak, "Law: Religious or Secular," 181.

Chapter 2

1. Sarah Stillman, "No Refuge," *New Yorker*, January 15, 2018, 32–43.

2. Possibly Tel Haror/Tel Hureirah, a major site and probable regional capital during the Middle Bronze Age and a more minor one during the Late Bronze Age.

3. All translations from the Bible and other ancient texts are mine, unless otherwise noted.

4. For such a view of Gen. 12:10–20, see Savina J. Teubal, "Sarah and Hagar: Matriarchs and Visionaries," in *A Feminist Companion to Genesis*, ed. Athalya Brenner (Sheffield: Sheffield Academic Press, 1997), 235–50.

5. As argued by Serge Frolov, "Sarah, Rebekah, and the Unchangeable Ruble: Unrecognized Folkloric Background of the 'Wife-Sister' Stories in Genesis," *Biblische Notizen* 150 (2011): 3–7.

6. Mignon R. Jacobs rightly notes that Abraham's "incessant focus on his well-being versus Sarah's gives the impression that Sarah has the power to control the course of his life." Mignon R. Jacobs, *Gender, Power, and Persuasion: The Genesis Narratives and Contemporary Portraits* (Grand Rapids: Baker Academic, 2007), 75.

7. The Hebrew *nabo' shomma* ("wherever we go") makes a pun on *nabi'* ("prophet"), a word play whose very clumsiness points to the contradictions built into Abraham's intercessory role in the story and the resolution of those conflicts by divine acceptance of the intermediation.

8. A helpful survey appears in Eunsoo Kim, "Minjung Theology in Korea: A Critique from a Reformed Theological Perspective," *Japan Christian Review* 64 (1998): 53–65.

9. This view is more widespread than just Genesis, of course. See, e.g., 1 Sam. 12:23; Amos 7:1–9; cf. Jer. 14:11–12.

10. Marcel Mauss, *The Gift*, trans. W. D. Halls, foreword by Mary Douglas (New York: Norton, 1990), 65.

11. Arjun Appadurai, "Introduction: Commodities and the Politics of Value,"

Notes

in *The Social Life of Things: Commodities in Cultural Perspective*, ed. Arjun Appadurai (Cambridge: Cambridge University Press, 1986), 21.

12. Great literature often draws upon the elements of oral storytelling, in which villains and heroes play clear-cut roles. The great artist, like the storytellers of the Pentateuch, bends those identities to reflect the complexity of life.

13. Claus Westermann, *Genesis 12–36*, trans. John J. Scullion, Continental Commentaries (Minneapolis: Fortress Press, 1995), 319.

14. Gen. 20:1–18 apparently comes from the Elohist, a literary stratum or "source" that has greater coherence than is sometimes assumed, as argued for by Joel S. Baden, *The Composition of the Pentateuch: Renewing the Documentary Hypothesis*, Anchor Yale Bible Reference Library (New Haven, CT: Yale University Press, 2012), 103–28. Baden notes that doublets in the Pentateuch "are not a mere collection of independent secondary additions, but are intricately and integrally connected on substantive narrative grounds" (125). For him this point applies to the constituent Pentateuchal sources and so argues against the supplementary/fragmentary hypotheses of Pentateuchal origins prevalent in contemporary European scholarship. However, in at least the case at hand, the repetition of the story must come from the final redactor or perhaps the Priestly source insofar as it was aware of the other versions, not the earlier sources themselves.

15. Note, however, the Septuagint and derivative versions, which shift the prepositional phrase *mimmena* ("from her") to the masculine (*mimmennu* = Greek *ex autou* = "from him"), making kingship derive from Isaac. Whatever the motivation of the change, the Masoretic Text provides the harder and therefore superior reading, consonant also with the prominence of the matriarch in the stories.

16. See Konrad Schmid, *Genesis and the Moses Story: Israel's Dual Origins in the Hebrew Bible*, trans. James D. Nogalski, Siphrut 3 (Winona Lake, IN: Eisenbrauns, 2010).

17. Theda Skocpol and Vanessa Williamson, *Tea Party and the Remaking of Republican Conservatism* (Oxford: Oxford University Press, 2012), 71–74.

Chapter 3

1. A good translation with brief notes appears in Miriam Lichtheim, *Ancient Egyptian Literature: A Book of Readings*, vol. 1: *The Old and Middle Kingdoms*, rev. ed., introduction by Antonio Loprieno (Berkeley: University of California Press, 2006), 222–35.

2. Lines 182–84 in Lichtheim, *Ancient Egyptian Literature*, 229.

3. Lines 290–95 in Lichtheim, *Ancient Egyptian Literature*, 233.

4. John Baines, "Interpreting Sinuhe," *Journal of Egyptian Archaeology* 68 (1982): 31–44, esp. 42.

5. A fine translation of Wenamun appears in William W. Hallo and K. Lawson

Younger, Jr., eds., *Canonical Compositions from the Biblical World*, vol. 1, *The Context of Scripture* (Leiden: Brill, 2003), 89–93.

6. Yairah Amit, "Travel Narratives and the Message of Genesis," in *The Formation of the Pentateuch: Bridging the Academic Cultures of Europe, Israel, and North America*, ed. Jan C. Gertz, Bernard M. Levinson, Dalit Rom-Shiloni, and Konrad Schmid (Tübingen: Mohr Siebeck, 2016), 242.

7. Accessible translations and helpful commentaries appear in Benjamin R. Foster, ed. and trans., *The Epic of Gilgamesh* (New York: Norton, 2001); and Andrew George, *The Epic of Gilgamesh* (New York: Penguin, 2003).

8. Noel K. Weeks, "Assyrian Imperialism and the Walls of Uruk," in *Gilgameš and the World of Assyria: Proceedings of the Conference Held at Mandelbaum House, the University of Sydney, 21–23 July 2004*, ed. Joseph Azize and Noel Weeks (Leuven: Peeters, 2007), 79–90; Amitai Baruchi-Unna, "Crossing the Boundaries: Literary Allusions to the Epic of Gilgamesh in the Account of Esarhaddon's Egyptian Campaign," in *Treasures on Camels' Humps: Historical and Literary Studies from the Ancient Near East Presented to Israel Eph'al*, ed. Mordechai Cogan and Dan'el Kahn (Jerusalem: Magnes, 2008), 54–65; but the epic itself may have had an anti-imperialist bent, as argued by Tracy Davenport, "An Anti-Imperialist Twist to the Gilgameš Epic," in Azize and Weeks, *Gilgameš and the World of Assyria*, 1–23.

9. For examples, see C. L. Seow, *Ecclesiastes*, Anchor Bible 18C (New York: Doubleday, 1997), 64–65.

10. Text 18 in Hayim Tadmor and Shigeo Yamada, eds., *The Royal Inscriptions of Tiglath-pileser III (744–727 BC), and Shalamaneser V (726–722 BC), Kings of Assyria*, Royal Inscriptions of the Neo-Assyrian Period 1 (Winona Lake, IN: Eisenbrauns, 2011), 55.

11. Herbert Donner and Wolfgang Röllig, *Kanaanäische und aramäische Inschriften*, 2nd ed. (Wiesbaden: Harrassowitz, 1966–1969), 24.

12. Donner and Röllig, *Kanaanäische und aramäische Inschriften*, 216.10–11.

13. A word play on the different meanings of cognate words (*šarru* and *śār*, *malku* and *melek*) in Akkadian versus Hebrew, as shown by several scholars, including Peter Machinist, "Assyria and Its Image in the First Isaiah," *Journal of the American Oriental Society* 103 (1983): 719–37.

14. For the careful balancing of the poetry of Nah. 3:9–11, see Duane L. Christensen, *Nahum*, Anchor Bible 24F (New Haven, CT: Yale University Press, 2009), 357–59. Nah. 2:8 (English 2:7) speaks of Nineveh, now feminized, as one who is "uncovered," playing on the dual meaning (or arguably, homonymous roots) of *galah* as "uncover" and "to exile," a line that 3:10 echoes.

15. Jer. 29:1, 4, 16, 20, 31.

16. Ezek. 1:1; 3:11, 15; 11:24, 25; 12:3, 4, 7, 11; 25:3.

17. Ezra 1:11; 2:1; 4:1; 6:19, 20, 21; 8:35; 9:4; 10:6, 7, 8, 16.

18. Cyril of Alexandria, *Commentary on the Twelve Prophets*, vol. 1, trans. Rob-

ert C. Hill, *The Fathers of the Church* 115 (Washington, DC: Catholic University of America Press, 2007), 214.

Chapter 4

1. A useful sampling of views and issues must include Donald B. Redford, *Egypt, Canaan, and Israel in Ancient Times* (Princeton, NJ: Princeton University Press, 1992); James Hoffmaier, *Israel in Egypt: The Evidence for the Authenticity of the Exodus Tradition* (Oxford: Oxford University Press, 1997); K. A. Kitchen, *On the Reliability of the Old Testament* (Grand Rapids: Eerdmans, 2003); and Richard Elliott Friedman, *The Exodus* (New York: HarperOne, 2017).

2. Peter Machinist, "Outsiders or Insiders: The Biblical View of Emergent Israel and Its Contexts," in *The Other in Jewish Thought and History*, ed. L. Silverstein and R. Cohn (New York: NYU Press, 1994), 35–60.

3. Note also the foreshadowing of the exodus story in Genesis (e.g., Gen. 15:13–14; 41:21; 50:24–25). The connections between the two origins stories go much further, in fact. As Thomas Römer points out, the portrayals of Abraham and Joseph, at least, make most sense as characters prefiguring Moses and his peers. See Thomas Römer, "Exodusmotive und Exoduspolemik in den Erzvätererzählung," in *Berührungspunkte: Studien zur Sozial- und Religionsgeschichte Israels und seiner Umwelt*, ed. Ingo Kottsieper, Rüdiger Schmitt, and Jakob Wöhrle, Alter Orient und Altes Testament 350 (Münster: Ugarit, 2008), 3–19.

4. That explicit argument does appear in Gen. 15:16, however.

5. Contrary to the arguments of Frank-Lothar Hossfeld and Erich Zenger, *Psalms 2: A Commentary on Psalms 51–100*, trans. Linda. M. Maloney, Hermeneia (Minneapolis: Fortress, 2005), 292–93.

6. David Novak, "Law: Religious or Secular?" *Tradition in the Public Square: A David Novak Reader*, ed. Randi Rashkover and Martin Kavka (Grand Rapids: Eerdmans, 2008), 177–81.

7. Tobit is a third-second century BCE book that Christians read as part of a secondary canon sometimes called the Apocrypha. For a brief introduction, see Otto Kaiser, *The Old Testament Apocrypha: An Introduction* (Peabody, MA: Hendrickson, 2004), 30–39.

Chapter 5

1. It is easy to multiply many examples of this phenomenon, as well as violations of it, which usually came in for criticism. See for example the treaty from the Syrian site of Sefire published in Joseph A. Fitzmyer, *The Aramaic Inscriptions of Sefire* (Rome: Pontifical Biblical Institute, 1995). A clear Israelite example of disgust

at royal sneakiness appears in 2 Kings 17:1-6, which faults the Israelite king Hoshea for breaking his treaty with Assyria itself. Perhaps he should never have made such a deal, but once made, a promise bears divine sanction. The one agreeing may not wriggle out of such a commitment, no matter how inconvenient it seems.

2. Amanda H. Podany, *Brotherhood of Kings: How International Relations Shaped the Ancient Near East* (Oxford: Oxford University Press, 2010), 10.

3. See James Bowman, *Honor: A History* (New York: Encounter, 2006).

4. Correctly, William H. C. Propp, *Exodus 1-18*, Anchor Bible 2 (New York: Doubleday, 1999), 132.

5. Edmund Wilson, *To the Finland Station: A Study in the Writing and Acting of History*, repr. ed. (New York: Macmillan, 1968), 380.

6. The phrase "uncircumcised lips" reflects a theme in prophetic call narratives, the inadequacy of the prophet for the task. Neither ordinary rhetorical skill nor ordinary moral character suffices for bridge-building between God and human beings, the role of the prophet.

7. The Hebrew word for "multitude, mob" appears rarely in the Hebrew Bible and usually denotes a group of foreign kings or their subjects (Jer. 25:20; 50:37; Ezek. 30:5). In one instance, however, it refers to non-Israelites who live among the Israelites (Neh. 13:3). That text offers an interesting counterbalance to the Exodus text and in doing so highlights the importance of the latter. Nehemiah's community faced extinction because of its numerical inferiority and tendency to merge into the surrounding cultures. So he and others worked to separate Israelites from the "multitude," especially in the context of worship. This and other moves in Ezra-Nehemiah seem to have been emergency measures that made sense under circumstances of crisis. Exodus 12, and indeed the rest of the Pentateuch, takes a much more open view toward non-Israelites living among the people. As the following chapter will show, Israelite law operated on the principle that non-Israelites could fully participate in worship of Yahweh (cf. also Isa. 56), provided they avoided worshiping other gods. Nehemiah's policy does not fit that larger, more tolerant picture, probably because of the special circumstances of his own time.

8. On this theme broadly, see Debra Scoggins Ballentine, *The Conflict Myth & the Biblical Tradition* (Oxford: Oxford University Press, 2015), esp. 92-97.

9. Adrienne Martin, *How We Hope: A Moral Psychology* (Princeton, NJ: Princeton University Press, 2014), 35.

10. Important discussions of Cyrus's reign appear in Amélie Kuhrt, "The Achaemenid Persian Empire (c. 550-c. 330 BCE): Continuities, Adaptations, Transformations," in *Empires*, ed. Susan E. Alcock, Terence N. D'Altroy, Kathleen D. Morrison, and Carla M. Sinopoli (Cambridge: Cambridge University Press, 2001), 93-123; Pierre Briant, *From Cyrus to Alexander: A History of the Persian Empire*, trans. Peter T. Daniels (Winona Lake, IN: Eisenbrauns, 2002), 31-61; and Matt Waters, "Parsumaš, Anšan, and Cyrus," in *Elam and Persia*, ed. Javier Álvarez-Mon (Winona Lake, IN: Eisenbrauns, 2011), 285-96.

Notes

11. Note the extensive discussion in A. Joseph Everson and Hyun Chul Paul Kim, eds., *The Desert Will Bloom: Poetic Visions in Isaiah*, Ancient Israel and Its Literature 4 (Atlanta: SBL, 2009).

Chapter 6

1. Joseph Story, *Commentaries on the Constitution of the United States*, 3 vols. (Boston: Hilliard, Gray, 1833), 1:384.

2. Note the discussion in Bernard M. Levinson, *Deuteronomy and the Hermeneutics of Legal Innovation* (Oxford: Oxford University Press, 1997). Whether these later revisions sought completely to displace the older laws is debatable, but in any case the Pentateuch included them all. This act of literary ecumenism reveals a unanimous interest in the welfare of migrants.

3. There is considerable evidence that the Covenant Code interacted directly or indirectly with Mesopotamian law, notably the much older Code of Hammurabi, and that the Israelite text sought not to create a comprehensive legal regime but to offer a more abstract, generalized approach to law. For the most elaborate and convincing form of this argument, see David P. Wright, *Inventing God's Law: How the Covenant Code of the Bible Used and Revised the Laws of Hammurabi* (Oxford: Oxford University Press, 2009).

4. Note the discussion in William H. C. Propp, *Exodus 19-40*, Anchor Bible 2A (New York: Doubleday, 2006), 258.

5. Perhaps the most sophisticated articulation of the economic view of the *gerim* to date appears in Christoph Bultmann, *Der Fremde im antiken Juda*, Forschungen zur Religion und Literatur des Alten und Neuen Testaments 153 (Göttingen: Vandenhoeck & Ruprecht, 1992).

6. In Deuteronomy's theology, Yahweh cannot dwell in a temple. So the temple becomes a symbol of the divine presence, albeit in a way unique on earth. So Deuteronomy expresses this complex idea of Yahweh being both present and not present by speaking of Yahweh's name residing in the place. Priestly texts like Exodus 40 and others describe a similar idea by speaking of the presence of Yahweh's "glory" in a place. That is, these texts all think that God cannot "be" somewhere in the same sense that a human being can be, since God is not limited by space and embodiment.

7. The Hebrew verb *nata* usually means to "stretch out," "bend," or "bend toward." Arguably, with *case* (Hebrew: *mishpat*) as an object, the verb could mean "subvert," hence "subvert justice"; see Richard D. Nelson, *Deuteronomy: A Commentary* (Louisville: Westminster John Knox, 2002), 292. The verb could also be translated more literally as "bend," that is, distort, as translated by Eckart Otto, *Deuteronomium 12-34*, vol. 2, *23, 16-34-12*, Herders Theologischer Kommentar zum Alten Testament (Freiburg im Breisgau: Herder, 2017), 1846. However, I prefer the

translation "stretch out" or "delay" because of the concern with prompt payment and management of resources in the surrounding verses. Justice delayed is justice denied, then and now.

8. In addition, Deut. 5:14 and 27:19 refer to the *gerim*, both texts originating in other legal collections that Deuteronomy absorbed, so to speak.

9. Scholars debate the dating of all the laws in Leviticus, with some laws and the practices they reflect seeming to come from the period before the Babylonian invasions, and others to come later. So some of Leviticus may date after Deuteronomy, and other parts before.

10. Deuteronomy and Leviticus also differ slightly on their conceptions of the holiness of the Israelite people and the implications of that holiness for practical behavior. See the discussion in Christiana van Houten, *The Alien in Israelite Law*, Journal for the Study of the Old Testament Supplement Series 107 (Sheffield: Sheffield Academic Press, 1991), 147-48.

11. Jacob Milgrom, *Leviticus 23-27*, Anchor Bible 3B (New York: Doubleday, 2001), 2187. The phrase *ger wetoshab* means "a migrant who has settled down," and is sometimes the preferred language of Leviticus and other priestly texts for referring to such people (see Gen. 23:4; Lev. 25:35, 45, 47; Num. 35:15). As in so many other cases, the vocabulary may change slightly from text to text, but the meaning remains closely similar.

12. For arguments for and against the historical existence of the Jubilee, see Robin J. DeWitt-Knauth, "The Jubilee Transformation: From Social Welfare to Hope of Restoration to Eschatological Salvation" (ThD diss., Harvard University, 2004).

Chapter 7

1. I thank the participants in the East-West Theological Forum, Seoul, Korea (May 7-9, 2015), who responded to an earlier version of this chapter and critiqued several of its points.

2. On the historical issues involved, see the discussion in William McKane, *A Critical and Exegetical Commentary on Jeremiah*, International Critical Commentary (Edinburgh: T&T Clark, 1996), 2:cxxxix-clx.

3. Cf. Jack R. Lundbom, *Jeremiah 21-36*, Anchor Bible 21B (New York: Doubleday, 2004), 344-48. On Hebrew epistolography, see Dennis Pardee, "An Overview of Ancient Hebrew Epistolography," *Journal of Biblical Literature* 97 (1978): 321-46; James Lindenberger, *Ancient Aramaic and Hebrew Letters*, Society of Biblical Literature Writings from the Ancient World 4 (Atlanta: Scholars Press, 1994), 1-12; Johannes Renz, *Die althebräischen Inschriften*, vol. 2, *Zusammenfassende Erörterungen*, *Paläographie und Glossar*, Handbuch der althebräischen Epigraphik 2/1 (Darmstadt: Wissenschaftliche Buchgesellschaft, 1995), 9-17.

Notes

4. See the rather schematic description of these developments in Rainer Albertz, *A History of Israelite Religion in the Old Testament Period*, vol. 2 of *From the Exile to the Maccabees*, trans. John E. Bowden (Louisville: Westminster John Knox, 1994), 370–87; with greater specificity, the studies in Oded Lipschits and Joseph Blenkinsopp, eds., *Judah and the Judeans in the Neo-Babylonian Period* (Winona Lake, IN: Eisenbrauns, 2003).

5. Note the seminal work of Bustenay Oded, *Mass Deportations and Deportees in the Neo-Assyrian Empire* (Wiesbaden: Reichert, 1979).

6. This creation theology is articulated in many priestly and Wisdom texts and most famously in the creation text of Genesis 1. There is no single Israelite creation theology, however, but rather a plurality of interlocking theologies. See the excellent survey in Othmar Keel and Silvia Schroer, *Creation: Biblical Theologies in the Context of the Ancient Near East*, trans. Peter T. Daniels (Winona Lake, IN: Eisenbrauns, 2015).

7. Indeed, the oracles against Babylon in Jer. 50–52 share the more negative view of empire that prevails in older texts such as Nahum and Zephaniah (against Assyria) and in Isaiah 40–55 against Babylonia.

8. See David S. Vanderhooft, *The Neo-Babylonian Empire and Babylon in the Latter Prophets*, Harvard Semitic Monographs 59 (Atlanta: Society of Biblical Literature, 1999); David S. Vanderhooft, "Babylonian Strategies of Imperial Control in the West: Royal Practice and Rhetoric," in Lipschits and Blenkinsopp, *Judah and the Judeans in the Neo-Babylonian Period*, 235–62.

9. Depending on one's reading of Jer. 13:19, which is a difficult text.

10. See also the detailed discussion of this theology of history by Louis Stulman, *Order and Chaos: Jeremiah as Symbolic Tapestry*, Biblical Seminar 57 (Sheffield: JSOT Press, 1998); Else Holt, "The Meaning of an Inclusio: A Theological Interpretation of the Book of Jeremiah MT," *Scandinavian Journal of the Old Testament* 17 (2003): 183–205 (who argues that the critique of Babylon is the key to understanding the entire Masoretic Text version of the book).

11. At some level, this claim reflects a theological agenda, not merely a factual description of a historical reality; note the discussion in, e.g., Gary N. Knoppers, Lester L. Grabbe, and Deirdre Fulton, eds., *Exile and Restoration Revisited: Essays on the Babylonian and Persian Periods in Memory of Peter R. Ackroyd*, Library of Second Temple Studies 73 (London: T&T Clark, 2009); Oded Lipschits, *The Fall and Rise of Jerusalem: Judah under Babylonian Rule* (Winona Lake, IN: Eisenbrauns, 2005).

12. On the problems of this verse, see McKane, *Jeremiah*, 2:855–56.

13. Cf. Hos. 11:1–11; 14:2–10 [English 1–9]; and the concluding oracle of each of the Minor Prophets.

14. For other uses of the phrase, see Deut. 30:3; Jer. 29:14; 30:3, 18; 31:23; 32:44; 33:7, 11, 26; 48:47; 49:6, 39; Ezek. 16:53; 29:14; 39:25; Hos. 6:11; Joel 4:11; Amos 9:14; Zech. 3:20; Pss. 14:7; 53:7; Job 42:10; Lam. 2:14. A classic study of the phrase

appears in Claus Westermann, *Prophetic Oracles of Salvation in the Old Testament*, trans. Keith Crim (Louisville: Westminster John Knox, 1991).

15. R. W. L. Moberly, *Prophecy and Discernment* (Cambridge: Cambridge University Press, 2006).

16. And at this level, his projections of history did not work out, since the Jewish community in southern Iraq flourished for more than 2,500 years.

17. On fasts, see the comments of Yair Hoffman, "The Fasts in the Book of Zechariah and the Fashioning of National Remembrance," in Lipschits and Blenkinsopp, *Judah and the Judeans in the Neo-Babylonian Period*, 169–218. Studies of the Deuteronomistic History's development and usage are extremely numerous. For good surveys of the current discussion, see Thomas Römer, *The So-Called Deuteronomistic History: A Sociological, Historical, and Literary Introduction* (London: T&T Clark, 2007); Mignon Jacobs and Raymond Person, Jr., eds., *Israelite Prophecy and the Deuteronomistic History: Portrait, Reality, and the Formation of a History* (Atlanta: Society of Biblical Literature, 2013).

18. Cornelia Wunsch, "Glimpses on the Lives of Deportees in Rural Babylonia," in *Arameans, Chaldeans, and Arabs in Babylonia and Palestine in the First Millennium B.C.*, ed. Angelika Berlejung and Michael P. Streck, Leipziger Altorientalistische Studien 3 (Wiesbaden: Harrassowitz, 2013), 247–60.

19. Sian Lazar, "Historical Narrative, Mundane Political Time, and Revolutionary Moments: Coexisting Temporalities in the Lived Experience of Social Movements," *Journal of the Royal Anthropological Institute* 20 (2014): 91–92.

20. An excellent description of such a reality appears in Gray Albert Abarca and Susan Bibler Coutin, "Sovereign Intimacies: The Lives of Documents within US State-Noncitizen Relationships," *American Ethnologist* 45 (2018): 7–19.

21. Paul Ricoeur, *Memory, History, Forgetting*, trans. Kathleen Blamey and David Pellauer (Chicago: University of Chicago Press, 2004), 43.

22. Jer. 33:9 apparently alludes to this very passage by using the vocabulary of "dread" (*pachad*) and "trembling" (*ragaz*), both part of the older text's vocabulary.

Chapter 8

1. International Organization for Migration, "World Migration Report 2018," November 2017, 304–5, http://publications.iom.int/system/files/pdf/wmr_2018_en .pdf.

2. Erhard Gerstenberger, *Israel in the Persian Period: The Fifth and Fourth Centuries B.C.E.*, trans. Siegfried Schatzmann (Atlanta: Society of Biblical Literature, 2011), 510.

3. NRSV's paraphrase "by flagons" misses the point, as does NIV's "by the king's command each guest was allowed to drink in his own way." NEB captures the verse

Notes

better with "the law of the drinking was that there should be no compulsion." Even better might be "the only rule about the drinking was that there should be no limit."

4. Jon Levenson has pointed out the connection between the Greek Esther's decree of Artaxerxes and a similar text attributed to the much later Egyptian ruler Ptolemy Philopater, as 3 Macc. 3:12-29 reports. See Jon Levenson, *Esther*, Old Testament Library (Louisville: Westminster John Knox, 1997), 75. In other words, Jews of the late Hellenistic period, say the second or first centuries BCE, recognized both the tendency of Gentile rulers to present themselves as wise and benevolent, and the unrealistic nature of that royal propaganda.

5. The book existed in several different versions in antiquity, indicating its popularity in diaspora communities. Many Christians consider it part of the Apocrypha or Deuterocanonical section of the Bible. Others regard it as simply an interesting and religiously valuable text. For a concise treatment of the historical, linguistic, and literary issues, see Joseph A. Fitzmyer, *Tobit*, Commentaries on Early Jewish Literature (Berlin: de Gruyter, 2003), esp. 1-28.

6. There are serious textual problems with this verse, and better manuscripts omit the third line above. See the discussion in Fitzmyer, *Tobit*, 311-12.

7. Following here the text of Manuscript B, from the twelfth century. See, however, the Greek translation of the Septuagint, which presents a very slightly different version.

Chapter 9

1. I have used the phrase "follower of Jesus" in lieu of the more common term *Christian* because a number of the earliest leaders of the church seem to have avoided the term. Paul, for example, never calls himself, his colleagues, or members of his churches "Christians," even though he spent a great deal of time in Antioch, the city in which, according to Acts, the name originated (Acts 11:26). Perhaps not much is at stake in this battle of vocabulary, and if the reader wishes to read "Christian" throughout this chapter, I make no objection. But perhaps choosing labels like "follower" or "disciple" reminds us that in the first century no one claimed to be a Christian in order to fit into a socially accepted group or to advance some mundane agenda. The label cost too much for that.

2. "Epistle to Diognetus" 5.4.

3. I leave to one side the controversial question of whether other early Christian Gospels, such as Thomas or Philip, also contain early material about Jesus. For thoughtful comments on the problem, see Christopher Tuckett, *From the Sayings to the Gospels*, Wissenschaftliche Untersuchungen zum Neuen Testament 328 (Tübingen: Mohr Siebeck, 2014), esp. 403-20.

4. Such a translation appears, for example, in Exod. 12:49; 20:10; 22:20; 23:9; Lev. 16:29; 17:8, 10, 13, 15; 18:26; 19:10; 19:34; 20:2; 22:18; 23:22; 24:16, 22; 25:23, 35,

47; Num. 9:14; 15:15, 16, 26, 29, 30, 19:10; Deut. 1:16; 5:14; 10:19; 14:29; 16:11, 14; 24:14, 17, 19; 26:11, 12, 13; 27:19; 29:10; 31:12.

5. See Thucydides, *History* 1.9.2; Xenophon, *Economics* 11.4. See also Job 20:26 Septuagint, where *epēlytos* renders the Hebrew *sarid*, "a fugitive."

6. Ruth 2:10; 2 Sam. (= 2 Reigns) 15:19; Ps. 68:8 (= Hebrew 69:9; English 69:8); Lam. 5:2; and Eccles. 6:2.

7. I am attracted by Gerd Theissen's arguments that Matthew's story reflects the same sort of military professionalism that Josephus attributes to soldiers resisting the schemes of the mad emperor Caligula. Theissen thinks that Matthew's source (Q) takes a positive view of the Roman army, or at least of some officers in it. See Gerd Theissen, *The Gospels in Context: Social and Political History in the Synoptic Tradition*, trans. Linda M. Maloney (Minneapolis: Fortress Press, 1991), 226–27.

8. Anne Applebaum, *Gulag: A History* (New York: Random House, 2003), 257.

9. For cautions on sacramentalism from a Roman Catholic perspective, see the somewhat astringent comments of Ralph Martin, "The Post-Christendom Sacramental Crisis: The Wisdom of Thomas Aquinas," *Nova et Vetera* 11 (2013): 57–75.

10. Matthew Levering, *Sacrifice and Community: Jewish Offering and Christian Eucharist*, Illuminations: Theory and Religion (Oxford: Blackwell, 2005), 199.

11. As in Gen. 15:13; Exod. 2:22; 18:3. In other texts, *paroikos* is a synonym for *prosēlytos*, usually translating part of a more elaborate Hebrew construction (Exod. 20:10; Lev. 25:23, 35, 47; Num. 35:15; Deut. 14:21; 23:8).

12. Shively T. J. Smith, *Strangers to Family: Diaspora and 1 Peter's Invention of God's Household* (Waco, TX: Baylor University Press, 2016), 165.

13. Paul A. Holloway, *Coping with Prejudice: 1 Peter in Social-Psychological Perspective*, Wissenschaftliche Untersuchungen zum Neuen Testament 244 (Tübingen: Mohr Siebeck, 2009).

Chapter 10

1. Ralph Drollinger, "What the Bible Says About Our Illegal Immigration Problem," Capitol Ministries, September 27, 2016, https://capmin.org/bible-says -illegal-immigration-problem-2 .

Bibliography

Abarca, Gray Albert, and Susan Bibler Coutin, "Sovereign Intimacies: The Lives of Documents within US State-Noncitizen Relationships." *American Ethnologist* 45 (2018): 7–19.

Albertz, Rainer. *A History of Israelite Religion in the Old Testament Period.* Vol. 2 of *From the Exile to the Maccabees.* Translated by John E. Bowden. Louisville: Westminster John Knox, 1994.

Amit, Yairah. "Travel Narratives and the Message of Genesis." In *The Formation of the Pentateuch: Bridging the Academic Cultures of Europe, Israel, and North America,* edited by Jan C. Gertz, Bernard M. Levinson, Dalit Rom-Shiloni, and Konrad Schmid, 223–42. Tübingen: Mohr Siebeck, 2016.

Appadurai, Arjun. "Introduction: Commodities and the Politics of Value." In *The Social Life of Things: Commodities in Cultural Perspective,* edited by Arjun Appadurai, 3–63. Cambridge: Cambridge University Press, 1986.

Applebaum, Anne. *Gulag: A History.* New York: Random House, 2003.

Baden, Joel S. *The Composition of the Pentateuch: Renewing the Doc-*

umentary Hypothesis. Anchor Yale Bible Reference Library. New Haven, CT: Yale University Press, 2012.

Baines, John. "Interpreting Sinuhe." *Journal of Egyptian Archaeology* 68 (1982): 31–44.

Ballentine, Debra Scoggins. *The Conflict Myth & the Biblical Tradition*. Oxford: Oxford University Press, 2015.

Baruchi-Unna, Amitai. "Crossing the Boundaries: Literary Allusions to the Epic of Gilgamesh in the Account of Esarhaddon's Egyptian Campaign." In *Treasures on Camels' Humps: Historical and Literary Studies from the Ancient Near East Presented to Israel Ephʿal*, edited by Mordechai Cogan and Danʾel Kahn, 54–65. Jerusalem: Magnes, 2008.

Bowman, James. *Honor: A History*. New York: Encounter, 2006.

Briant, Pierre. *From Cyrus to Alexander: A History of the Persian Empire*. Translated by Peter T. Daniels. Winona Lake, IN: Eisenbrauns, 2002.

Bultmann, Christoph. *Der Fremde im antiken Juda*. Forschungen zur Religion und Literatur des Alten und Neuen Testaments 153. Göttingen: Vandenhoeck & Ruprecht, 1992.

Christensen, Duane L. *Nahum*. AB 24F. New Haven, CT: Yale University Press, 2009.

Cyril of Alexandria. *Commentary on the Twelve Prophets*. Vol. 2. Translated by Robert C. Hill. The Fathers of the Church 115. Washington, DC: Catholic University of America Press, 2007.

Davenport, Tracy. "An Anti-Imperialist Twist to the Gilgameš Epic." In *Gilgameš and the World of Assyria: Proceedings of the Conference held at Mandelbaum House, the University of Sydney, 21–23 July 2004*, edited by Joseph Azize and Noel Weeks, 1–23. Leuven: Peeters, 2007.

DeWitt-Knauth, Robin J. "The Jubilee Transformation: From Social Welfare to Hope of Restoration to Eschatological Salvation." ThD diss., Harvard University, 2004.

Everson, A. Joseph, and Hyun Chul Paul Kim, eds. *The Desert Will Bloom: Poetic Visions in Isaiah*. Ancient Israel and Its Literature 4. Atlanta: Society of Biblical Literature, 2009.

Friedman, Richard Elliott. *The Exodus*. New York: HarperOne, 2017.

Fitzgerald, Frances. *The Evangelicals: The Struggle to Shape America.* New York: Simon and Schuster, 2017.

Fitzmyer, Joseph A. *The Aramaic Inscriptions of Sefire.* Rome: Pontifical Biblical Institute, 1995.

———. *Tobit.* Commentaries on Early Jewish Literature. Berlin: de Gruyter, 2003.

Foster, Benjamin R., ed. and trans. *The Epic of Gilgamesh.* New York: Norton, 2001.

Frolov, Serge. "Sarah, Rebekah, and the Unchangeable Ruble: Unrecognized Folkloric Background of the 'Wife-Sister' Stories in Genesis." *Biblische Notizen* 150 (2011): 3-7.

George, Andrew. *The Epic of Gilgamesh.* New York: Penguin, 2003.

Gerstenberger, Erhard. *Israel in the Persian Period: The Fifth and Fourth Centuries B.C.E.* Translated by Siegfried Schatzmann. Atlanta: Society of Biblical Literature, 2011.

Hoffmaier, James. *Israel in Egypt: The Evidence for the Authenticity of the Exodus Tradition.* Oxford: Oxford University Press, 1997.

Hoffman, Yair. "The Fasts in the Book of Zechariah and the Fashioning of National Remembrance." In *Judah and the Judeans in the Neo-Babylonian Period,* edited by Oded Lipschits and Joseph Blenkinsopp, 169-218. Winona Lake, IN: Eisenbrauns, 2003.

Holloway, Paul A. *Coping with Prejudice: 1 Peter in Social-Psychological Perspective.* Wissenschaftliche Untersuchungen zum Neuen Testament 244. Tübingen: Mohr Siebeck, 2009.

Holt, Else. "The Meaning of an Inclusio: A Theological Interpretation of the Book of Jeremiah MT." *Scandinavian Journal of the Old Testament* 17 (2003): 183-205.

Jacobs, Mignon R. *Gender, Power, and Persuasion: The Genesis Narratives and Contemporary Portraits.* Grand Rapids: Baker Academic, 2007.

Jacobs, Mignon, and Raymond Person, Jr., eds. *Israelite Prophecy and the Deuteronomistic History: Portrait, Reality, and the Formation of a History.* Atlanta: Society of Biblical Literature, 2013.

Kaiser, Otto. *The Old Testament Apocrypha: An Introduction.* Peabody, MA: Hendrickson, 2004.

Keel, Othmar, and Silvia Schroer. *Creation: Biblical Theologies in the Context of the Ancient Near East.* Translated by Peter T. Daniels. Winona Lake, IN: Eisenbrauns, 2015.

Kim, Eunsoo. "Minjung Theology in Korea: A Critique from a Reformed Theological Perspective." *Japan Christian Review* 64 (1998): 53-65.

Kitchen, K. A. *On the Reliability of the Old Testament.* Grand Rapids: Eerdmans, 2003.

Knoppers, Gary N., Lester L. Grabbe, and Deirdre Fulton, eds. *Exile and Restoration Revisited: Essays on the Babylonian and Persian Periods in Memory of Peter R. Ackroyd.* Library of Second Temple Studies 73. London: T&T Clark, 2009.

Kuhrt, Amélie. "The Achaemenid Persian Empire (c. 550–c. 330 BCE): Continuities, Adaptations, Transformations." In *Empires,* edited by Susan E. Alcock, Terence N. D'Altroy, Kathleen D. Morrison, and Carla M. Sinopoli, 93-123. Cambridge: Cambridge University Press, 2001.

Lazar, Sian. "Historical Narrative, Mundane Political Time, and Revolutionary Moments: Coexisting Temporalities in the Lived Experience of Social Movements." *Journal of the Royal Anthropological Institute* 20 (2014): 91-108.

Levenson, Jon. *Esther.* Old Testament Library. Louisville: Westminster John Knox, 1997.

Levering, Matthew. *Sacrifice and Community: Jewish Offering and Christian Eucharist.* Illuminations: Theory and Religion. Oxford: Blackwell, 2005.

Levinson, Bernard M. *Deuteronomy and the Hermeneutics of Legal Innovation.* Oxford: Oxford University Press, 1997.

Lichtheim, Miriam. *The Old and Middle Kingdoms.* Vol. 1 of *Ancient Egyptian Literature: A Book of Readings.* Revised ed. Introduction by Antonio Loprieno. Berkeley: University of California Press, 2006.

Lindenberger, James. *Ancient Aramaic and Hebrew Letters.* Society of Biblical Literature Writings from the Ancient World 4. Atlanta: Scholars Press, 1994.

Lipschits, Oded, and Joseph Blenkinsopp, eds. *Judah and the Judeans in the Neo-Babylonian Period.* Winona Lake, IN: Eisenbrauns, 2003.

Lucassen, Jan, and Leo Lucassen. "Migrations, Migration History, History: Old Paradigms and New Perspectives." In *Migrations, Migration History, History: Old Paradigms and New Perspectives,* edited by Jan Lucassen and Leo Lucassen, 9-38. Bern: Peter Lang, 1999.

Lundbom, Jack R. *Jeremiah 21-36.* AB 21B. New York: Doubleday, 2004.

Machinist, Peter. "Assyria and Its Image in the First Isaiah." *Journal of the American Oriental Society* 103 (1983): 719-37.

———. "Outsiders or Insiders: The Biblical View of Emergent Israel and Its Contexts." In *The Other in Jewish Thought and History,* edited by L. Silverstein and R. Cohn, 35-60. New York: NYU Press, 1994.

Martin, Adrienne. *How We Hope: A Moral Psychology.* Princeton, NJ: Princeton University Press, 2014.

Martin, Ralph. "The Post-Christendom Sacramental Crisis: The Wisdom of Thomas Aquinas." *Nova et Vetera* 11 (2013): 57-75.

Mauss, Marcel. *The Gift.* Translated by W. D. Halls. Foreword by Mary Douglas. New York: Norton, 1990.

McKane, William. *A Critical and Exegetical Commentary on Jeremiah.* International Critical Commentary. 2 vols. Edinburgh: T&T Clark, 1996.

Milgrom, Jacob. *Leviticus 23-27.* AB 3B. New York: Doubleday, 2001.

Moberly, R. W. L. *Prophecy and Discernment.* Cambridge: Cambridge University Press, 2006.

Nelson, Richard D. *Deuteronomy: A Commentary.* Louisville: Westminster John Knox, 2002.

Novak, David. *Tradition in the Public Square: A David Novak Reader.* Edited by Randi Rashkover and Martin Kavka. Grand Rapids: Eerdmans, 2008.

Oded, Bustenay. *Mass Deportations and Deportees in the Neo-Assyrian Empire.* Wiesbaden: Reichert, 1979.

Otto, Eckart. *Deuteronomium 12-34,* vol. 2, *23, 16-34-12.* Herders Theologischer Kommentar zum Alten Testament. Freiburg im Breisgau: Herder, 2017.

Pardee, Dennis. "An Overview of Ancient Hebrew Epistolography." *Journal of Biblical Literature* 97 (1978): 321–46.

Podany, Amanda H. *Brotherhood of Kings: How International Relations Shaped the Ancient Near East*. Oxford: Oxford University Press, 2010.

Propp, William H. C. *Exodus 1–18*. AB 2. New York: Doubleday, 1999.

Redford, Donald B. *Egypt, Canaan, and Israel in Ancient Times*. Princeton, NJ: Princeton University Press, 1992.

Renz, Johannes. *Zusammenfassende Erörterungen, Paläographie und Glossar*. Vol. 2 of *Die althebräischen Inschriften*. Handbuch der althebräischen Epigraphik 2/1. Darmstadt: Wissenschaftliche Buchgesellschaft, 1995.

Ricoeur, Paul. *Memory, History, Forgetting*. Translated by Kathleen Blamey and David Pellauer. Chicago: University of Chicago Press, 2004.

Römer, Thomas. "Exodusmotive und Exoduspolemik in den Erzvätererzählung." In *Berührungspunkte: Studien zur Sozial- und Religionsgeschichte Israels und seiner Umwelt*, edited by Ingo Kottsieper, Rüdiger Schmitt, and Jakob Wöhrle, 3–19. Alter Orient und Altes Testament 350. Münster: Ugarit, 2008.

———. *The So-Called Deuteronomistic History: A Sociological, Historical, and Literary Introduction*. London: T&T Clark, 2007.

Schmid, Konrad. *Genesis and the Moses Story: Israel's Dual Origins in the Hebrew Bible*. Translated by James D. Nogalski. Siphrut 3. Winona Lake, IN: Eisenbrauns, 2010.

Seow, C. L. *Ecclesiastes*. AB 18C. New York: Doubleday, 1997.

Skocpol, Theda, and Vanessa Williamson. *The Tea Party and the Remaking of Republican Conservatism*. Oxford: Oxford University Press, 2012.

Smith, Shively T. J. *Strangers to Family: Diaspora and 1 Peter's Invention of God's Household*. Waco, TX: Baylor University Press, 2016.

Stillman, Sarah. "No Refuge." *New Yorker*, January 15, 2018, 32–43.

Story, Joseph. *Commentaries on the Constitution of the United States*. 3 vols. Boston: Hilliard, Gray, 1833.

Strawn, Brent A. *The Old Testament Is Dying: A Diagnosis and Recommended Treatment*. Grand Rapids: Baker Academic, 2017.

Stulman, Louis. *Order and Chaos: Jeremiah as Symbolic Tapestry*. The Biblical Seminar 57. Sheffield: JSOT Press, 1998.

Tadmor, Hayim, and Shigeo Yamada, eds. *The Royal Inscriptions of Tiglath-pileser III (744-727 BC), and Shalamaneser V (726-722 BC), Kings of Assyria*. Royal Inscriptions of the Neo-Assyrian Period 1. Winona Lake, IN: Eisenbrauns, 2011.

Teubal, Savina J. "Sarah and Hagar: Matriarchs and Visionaries." In *A Feminist Companion to Genesis*, edited by Athalya Brenner, 235-50. Sheffield: Sheffield Academic Press, 1997.

Theissen, Gerd. *The Gospels in Context: Social and Political History in the Synoptic Tradition*. Translated by Linda M. Maloney. Minneapolis: Fortress Press, 1991.

Tuckett, Christopher. *From the Sayings to the Gospels*. Wissenschaftliche Untersuchungen zum Neuen Testament 328. Tübingen: Mohr Siebeck, 2014.

Vanderhooft, David S. "Babylonian Strategies of Imperial Control in the West: Royal Practice and Rhetoric." In *Judah and the Judeans in the Neo-Babylonian Period*, edited by Oded Lipschits and Joseph Blenkinsopp, 235-62. Winona Lake, IN: Eisenbrauns, 2003.

————. *The Neo-Babylonian Empire and Babylon in the Latter Prophets*. Harvard Semitic Monographs 59. Atlanta: SBL, 1999.

van Houten, Christiana. *The Alien in Israelite Law*. Journal for the Study of the Old Testament Supplement Series 107. Sheffield: Shcf field Academic Press, 1991.

Waters, Matt. "Parsumaš, Anšan, and Cyrus." In *Elam and Persia*, edited by Javier Álvarez-Mon, 285-96. Winona Lake, IN: Eisenbrauns, 2011.

Weeks, Noel K. "Assyrian Imperialism and the Walls of Uruk." In *Gilgameš and the World of Assyria: Proceedings of the Conference Held at Mandelbaum House, the University of Sydney, 21-23 July 2004*, edited by Joseph Azize and Noel Weeks, 79-90. Leuven: Peeters, 2007.

Westermann, Claus. *Genesis 12-36*. Translated by John J. Scullion. Continental Commentaries. Minneapolis: Fortress Press, 1995.

————. *Prophetic Oracles of Salvation in the Old Testament*. Trans. Keith Crim. Louisville: Westminster John Knox, 1991.

Wilson, Edmund. *To the Finland Station: A Study in the Writing and Acting of History.* Reprint ed. New York: Macmillan, 1968.

Wright, David P. *Inventing God's Law: How the Covenant Code of the Bible Used and Revised the Laws of Hammurabi.* Oxford: Oxford University Press, 2009.

Wunsch, Cornelia. "Glimpses on the Lives of Deportees in Rural Babylonia." In *Arameans, Chaldeans, and Arabs in Babylonia and Palestine in the First Millennium B.C.*, edited by Angelika Berlejung and Michael P. Streck, 247–60. Leipziger Altorientalistische Studien 3. Wiesbaden: Harrassowitz, 2013.

Index

Abimelek: claim of innocence, 16, 18-19; and gift giving, 22-23; intercession for, 21-22, 23-24; role as protector, 26

Abraham and Sarah: and complexity of Genesis migration stories, 25-27; defense as migrants, 19-21; in epistle to Hebrews, 137-38; fears of migration validated, 24-25; and gift giving, 22-23; intercession for Abimelek, 21-22, 23-24, 148n7; migration to Gerar, 16

Ahasuerus, King of Persia, 114-16

Alexander the Great, 119

Amit, Yairah, 35

Ammonites, 87-88

Amos, 41, 43, 49-51

ancient Near East: deportation practices, 37-42, 99; Egyptian stories of migration, 31-35; golah concept, 40-43; Mesopotamian stories of migration, 36-37; Persian Empire, 75, 114-16, 119;

Seleucid dynasty, 119-20. See also diaspora; exodus and exile

Antiochus IV Epiphanes, 119-20

Appadurai, Arjun, 23

Applebaum, Anne, 132

Arendt, Hannah, 72

Assyrian Empire, 37 40, 117

attritional time, 108

Babylonian Empire: deportation practices, 41-42, 99; negative prophetic view of, 103, 155n7, 155n10

Babylonian Exile: commitment to shalom during, 101-4; as divine gift, 104-6; Jeremiah's letters during, 99-100; and theological view of identity, 106-10

Baden, Joel S., 149n14

Baines, John, 33

baptism, 134

biblical migration experience: in Esther, 108, 114-17, 157n4; golah concept, 40-43, 150n14;

as learning opportunity, 44–45; parallels with ancient Near East stories, 35–36, 37; in Psalms, 51–53; as source for understanding modern migration, 8–9, 143–45; themes, 16–18; in Tobit, 61, 108, 117–19, 151n7, 157n5. *See also* Exodus (book); Genesis; historical texts; legal texts; New Testament; prophetic texts

Bir-rakib, 39

Book of Consolation, 105–6

Bultmann, Christoph, 153n5

Capitol Ministries, 142

centurion story, 129–32

Christianity. *See* early church

church: and Religious Right, 3–5, 142–43; responsibilities regarding migration legislation, 10–12, 144–45. *See also* early church

collective memory: connection to empathy, 64; and identity, 106–10; of Israel's migration story, 47–49

Covenant Code, 83–86, 153n3

creation theology, 102–3, 155n6

cultural superiority, 34–35

Cyril of Alexandria, 44–45

Cyrus, King of Persia, 75, 103

Daniel, 119–22

David, King, 66–67

Decalogue, 91–93

deportation, practices of, 37–42, 99. *See also* diaspora; exodus and exile

Deuteronomistic History, 54, 108

Deuteronomy, 86–91, 153n6, 154n8, 154n10

diaspora: in Daniel, 119–22; in Esther, 114–17, 157n4; identity formation in, 122–23; during Second Temple period, 114; as term, 113–14; texts on Jewish behavior in, 108; in Tobit,

117–19, 157n5. *See also* exodus and exile

dietary laws, 86–87, 94

early church: "Christian" as term, 157n1; model of Jesus's acceptance of strangers, 5–6, 128–32; Paul's unified and inclusive vision for, 133–37; self-conception grounded in Old Testament migration experience, 124–26, 137–39

economic model, of *gerim*, 85–86

Egypt: and Egyptians in Israelite law, 88; Israelite migration experience in, 68–72, 78–80; overview of Exodus story, 64–65; pharaoh in Exodus story, 66, 67–68, 71–72; stories of migration, 31–35

empathy, 3, 4, 59, 64, 80, 85, 143

Enmerkar, 36

Ephesians, 136–37

Epistle to Diognetus, 126

Esther, 108, 114–17, 157n4

Eucharist, 134

Exodus (book): complexity of, 71–72, 78–80; interactions between Moses and God, 70–71; oppressed migrants, 68–69; overview, 64–65; pharaoh as tyrant, 66, 67–68, 71–72

exodus and exile: in Amos, 49–51; and commitment to *shalom*, 101–4; complexity in stories of, 71–72, 78–80, 152n7; connection to Genesis, 28, 151n3; deportation practices in Near East, 37–42, 99; as divine gift, 104–6; *golah* concept, 40–43; in historical texts, 54–55; in Isaiah, 55–57, 74–78; Israel's collective memory of, 47–49; and mutual obligations between Israel and God, 58–60; in Nehemiah, 57–58; omissions in stories of,

61–62; in Psalms, 51–53; and
theological view of identity,
106–10. *See also* diaspora
Ezekiel, 42
Ezra, 42

festival laws, 87
1 Corinthians, 133–34
1 Kings, 54–55
1 Peter, 138–39
food laws, 86–87, 94
forced migration, practices of,
37–42, 99. *See also* diaspora;
exodus and exile

Genesis: and biblical themes on
migration, 16–18; complexity of
migration stories, 25–27, 149n12,
149n14; and danger of migration, 24–25, 26; and gift-giving
culture, 22–23; Joseph story,
34–35; tension and mediation in
Abraham and Abimelek story,
16, 18–22, 23–24
Gentiles: Jesus's acceptance of,
129–32; Paul's letters to, 133–37;
shared identity with Jews,
138–39
ger (migrant/alien): in Covenant
Code, 83–86; in Deuteronomy,
86–91, 154n8; in priestly laws,
93–96; in Ten Commandments,
91–93; terminology, 83, 127–28,
137, 138, 154n11
Gerstenberger, Erhard, 114
gift giving, 22–23
Gilgamesh, 36–37
God: complexity of, 72; designation in Jeremiah, 101–2; gift of
shalom, 104–6; interactions with
Moses, 70–71; intervention in
Abraham and Abimelek story,
16, 18–19, 21–22, 24–25; presence
of, 153n6; roles in Israel's migration story, 51–52, 54–55, 57–60,
75–78, 121

golah concept, 40–43, 150n14
Grotius, Hugo, 11–12
gur (to be a migrant or sojourner),
16

Haman, 114–16
han (unresolved bitterness against
gratuitous suffering), 21
Hebrew Bible. *See* biblical migration experience
Hebrews (book), 126, 137–38
heroic traveler stories, 36–37
historical texts: conceptions of
exodus and exile, 54–55; Deuteronomistic History, 54, 108; *golah*
concept, 41–42; on loyalty of
rulers, 66–67
historical time, 108
historical understanding, and
identity, 106–10
Hobbes, Thomas, 12
Holloway, Paul, 139
Holt, Else, 155n10
hope, as concept, 73–74
Hosea, 44–45
hosts. *See* rulers and the state

identity: formation in diaspora,
122–23; and historical understanding, 106–10; shared between Gentiles and Jews, 138–39
immigration. *See* migration and
immigration
intermarriage, 88, 101, 102
Isaiah: complexity of, 78–80;
conception of exodus and exile,
39–40, 55–57, 74–78; vision of
renewed world, 103–4
Israelites, as host of migrants. *See*
legal texts
Israelites, as migratory people. *See*
diaspora; Exodus (book); exodus
and exile; Genesis

Jacobs, Mignon R., 148n6
Jeremiah: on commitment to

shalom, 101–4; on divine gift of
shalom, 104–6; *golah* concept in,
42; influence on Daniel, 120;
letters to deportees, 99–100; view
of history and identity, 106–10
Jesus, 5–6, 128–32
Joseph, 34–35
Josephus, 158n7

Kilamuwa, 39

labor laws, 88–89, 91–92
landholding, 94–95
law. *See* legal texts
Lazar, Sian, 108
legal texts: collections in Bible,
82–83, 153n2; Covenant Code,
83–86, 153n3; derived from
human interconnectedness, 72;
in Deuteronomy, 86–91, 154n8;
interpretation of, 81–82, 91;
priestly laws, 93–96; Ten Commandments, 91–93
Levenson, Jon, 157n4
Levering, Matthew, 134
Leviticus, 93–96, 154nn9-10
liturgical texts, 51–53
loyalty, of rulers, 66–67
Luke, 129–32
Luther, Martin, 81

marriage, 88, 101, 102
Martin, Adrienne, 73–74
Marx, Karl, 68
Matthew, 128–32, 158n7
Mauss, Marcel, 22
memory. *See* collective memory
Mesopotamia. *See* ancient Near
East
migration and immigration: Bible
as source for understanding,
8–9, 143–45; statistics and leg-
islative history, 6–8, 147n6. *See
also* biblical migration experience; diaspora; exodus and exile
Milgrom, Jacob, 94–95

Moabites, 87–88
moral responsibility, 46–47, 53,
54–55, 57–60, 79–80
Moses, 69, 70–71
multitude of non-Israelites, 72,
152n7

Nahum, 40, 41, 150n14
Near East. *See* ancient Near East
Nebuchadnezzar, 41–42, 53
Nehemiah, 57–58, 152n7
New Testament: influenced by Old
Testament migrant experience,
125–26, 137–39; Jesus as stranger
and host of strangers, 5–6,
128–32; Pauline letters, 133–37;
terminology for migrants, 127–28
Novak, David, 11–12, 60, 139
Numbers, 96

offerings, 87, 90
Old Testament. *See* biblical migration experience
orphans, 84, 86, 87, 89

parepidēmoi (sojourner), 138
Passover, 96
Paul, Apostle, 133 37
Pentateuch, 149n14. *See also* Exodus
(book); Genesis; legal texts
Pentecost, 87
Persian Empire, 75, 114–16, 119
pharaoh (Exodus story), 66, 67–68,
71–72
phenomenology of human agreement, 12, 60
Podany, Amanda, 67
poverty, 85–86
priestly laws, 93–96
property ownership, 94–95
prophetic texts: on commitment
to *shalom*, 101–4; conceptions
of exodus and exile, 39–40, 43,
49–51, 55–58, 74–78; diaspora
in Daniel, 119–22; on divine gift
of *shalom*, 104–6; *golah* concept,